A Mysterious Life and Calling

THE NOTED AND FAMOUS

REV. MRS. C. S. RILEY

OF

LINCOLNVILLE. S. C.

A Mysterious Life and Calling

FROM SLAVERY TO MINISTRY IN SOUTH CAROLINA

Reverend Mrs. Charlotte S. Riley

Edited with an introduction by
Crystal J. Lucky

THE UNIVERSITY OF WISCONSIN PRESS

The University of Wisconsin Press
1930 Monroe Street, 3rd Floor
Madison, Wisconsin 53711-2059
uwpress.wisc.edu

3 Henrietta Street, Covent Garden
London WCE 8LU, United Kingdom
eurospanbookstore.com

Printed in the United States of America

This book may be available in a digital edition.

Library of Congress Cataloging-in-Publication Data

Riley, Charlotte S., 1839-, author.
A mysterious life and calling: from slavery to ministry in South Carolina /
Reverend Mrs. Charlotte S. Riley; edited with an introduction by Crystal J. Lucky.
pages   cm. — (Wisconsin studies in autobiography)
Includes bibliographical references and index.
ISBN 978-0-299-30674-8 (pbk.: alk. paper)
1. Riley, Charlotte S., 1839-.   2. African American women—South Carolina—Biography.
3. African American women clergy—South Carolina—Biography.
4. Women slaves—South Carolina—Biography.   5. Freedmen—South Carolina—Biography.
6. African Methodist Episcopal Church. South Carolina Conference—Clergy—Biography.
I. Lucky, Crystal J., editor, writer of introduction.   II. Title.
III. Series: Wisconsin studies in autobiography.
E185.97.R55   2016
287'.8092—dc23
[B]
2015010199

CONTENTS

FOREWORD

Joycelyn K. Moody

At the turn of the twenty-first century, I wrote first a doctoral dissertation on nineteenth-century black women's autobiographies and then a monograph on black women's spiritual narratives. If I were writing those works today, I could do so in a considerably richer, more varied landscape of sacred, cultural, and critical printed discourses. I would be especially exhilarated to work with Crystal Lucky's edition of *A Mysterious Life and Calling: From Slavery to Ministry in South Carolina* by Reverend Mrs. Charlotte S. Riley. Riley's book (originally titled *The Autobiography: A Mysterious Life and Calling*) expands the late twentieth-century era of intensive recovery of both black women's writings from the nineteenth century and what has been called a kind of renaissance of 1970s contemporary black women's writings, both imaginative and critical. For *A Mysterious Life and Calling* tells an exceptional story of a black woman licensed—literally and figuratively—to speak to audiences composed of diverse persons. As it is, however, Riley's *Mysterious Life and Calling* emerges in a very significant moment today, one of black print culture studies as well as renewed interest in black Southern writings—secular, sacred, cultural, and provocative. We are fortunate indeed that Crystal Lucky's response to a dare has yielded a rich resource, one to the occasion of which Lucky has brilliantly risen.

What follows this foreword, then, is a book encompassing *two* black women's achievements: Lucky's insightful amplification of a heretofore lost-in-the-archives gem and Riley's adroit reconstruction of her life of truths and triumphs. Riley succeeds admirably, forming *A Mysterious Life and Calling* into a narrative detailing her pioneering life as a Presbyterian converting to a sanctified

Methodism and as a devout woman called to preach in a black virulently patriarchal church denomination. Furthermore, her autobiography documents her life as an educator in postbellum South Carolina schools for indigent formerly enslaved peoples, as an itinerant minister across the enslaved then newly emancipated South, and as a shrewd, intelligent businesswoman determined to help sharecroppers avoid economic disenfranchisement at the hands of corrupt Southern white supremacists. Moreover, Riley's autobiography traces her journeys as a once-married single woman eventually in the steady, faithful company of a few particular Christian sister-companions.

Often breathtaking, Riley's story compels our attention as well as our reconsideration of African American literary and cultural traditions. Contemporary readers interested in women's and gender studies will appreciate Riley's *Mysterious Life and Calling*, for Riley's revelations about her life as a black woman involved in many religious, political, educational, cultural, and institutional contexts. There is a great deal to marvel at in the autobiography along these lines, and contemplating them helps us gain entry into the richer depths of the text.

Riley takes her place among other African American women Christian preachers of her era and since. Her account of her determination to work as a minister among other black women and men Christian exhorters and preachers of the nineteenth century expands our understanding of gender norms during the years of her lifetime, and of (black) women's attitudes toward those standards, for Riley carefully delineates myriad aspects of her life and her intersectional identity and experiences. She reveals her awareness that what happened to her in any given situation simply could not or would not have happened in precisely the same way were her social locations and identity different. In addition, Riley's portrayals of the gender-and denomination-based challenges to her ministry help us appreciate the strategies she employed to overcome Black Church chauvinisms as practiced by both African American men and women. Furthermore, her anecdotes about her religious devotion and her vigorous ministry often mention her dependence on her women colleagues, thereby illuminating ways nineteenth-century black holy women supported each other to ensure the physical safety, emotional support, and pragmatic sustenance vital to all throughout their itinerant ministries.

Significantly, Riley's autobiography reveals a world of southern AME women evangelists heretofore unrecognized in academic black letters. In terms of black women's spiritual labors, Lucky situates *A Mysterious Life and Calling* amid other African American women's spiritual autobiographies such as *The Life and Religious Experience of Jarena Lee, a Coloured Lady, Giving an Account of Her*

Call to Preach the Gospel (1836). Indeed, Lucky's restoration of Riley's spiritual narrative reforms the trajectory and genealogy of ministerial writings by US black women and men published during the middle of the nineteenth century. Before the important recovery event that Riley's *Mysterious Life and Calling* constitutes, scholars had no evidence of a black (woman's) spiritual autobiography produced in the US South during the pre–Civil War years and extending into—and beyond—Reconstruction. Riley names and Lucky specifies some of the foremost figures of the African Methodist Episcopal (AME) Church, including Bishop Daniel Payne, members of the AME Book Concern, and a number of Riley's black preacherly sisters.[1]

As Lucky details, Riley's ministry joins a tradition of black women preachers signaled and celebrated by William L. Andrews's *Sisters of the Spirit* (1986) and Dorothy Sterling's *We Are Your Sisters* (1997) and composed of such forceful African American holy women writers as Amanda Berry Smith, Rebecca Cox Jackson, Zilpha Elaw, Julia Foote, Jarena Lee, Nancy Prince, Maria W. Stewart, and Sojourner Truth. While some of these pious women have remained consistently available (if not also exactly in the public eye) since their earliest public exertions, their writings and/or writings about them in the last decades of the twentieth century brought them into our consciousness in renewed ways. Like many of these women's heteronormative marriages, too, Riley's works best for her when it is no more, ended by de facto divorce or spousal death or some other form of dismantling. Riley's rhetorical handling of her own unhappy marriage expresses her striking discursive skill. From youth, her religious conviction and her determination to respond positively to a divine calling expose her to gender-based challenges as daughter, spouse, and colleague that will be familiar to readers of writings by women Carla Peterson has included in *"Doers of the Word."* African American families and the living conditions of enslaved black people in Charleston, South Carolina, during the antebellum years emerge as extraordinary subjects in *A Mysterious Life and Calling*, especially given Lucky's scrupulous attention to Riley's text and contexts.

One of the most exhilarating aspects of Riley's autobiograhy is its displacement of Harriet Jacobs's *Incidents in the Life of a Slave Girl* as the lone autobiographical account of an enslaved antebellum black (or rather, black and white) woman's life *"Written by Herself."* That is, while we have had access to accounts of enslaved antebellum black women's lives in bondage as they narrated them to a variety of kinds of interlocutors, from novelists such as Harriet Beecher Stowe to abolitionists such as Olive Gilbert, Jacobs has held the ambiguous honor of remaining the only known enslaved woman to inscribe her life story while slavery still ruled as the law of the land.[2] Now, thanks to Professor Lucky, we can read comparatively, and understand more completely bound black womanhood as written by herself from the perspective of another forthright and skillful African American woman born into bondage in the Carolinas. To be sure, the most superficial differences between Jacobs's reconstruction of her life and Riley's offer opportunities for complex and robust examination.

For one thing, Riley's relationships with white Southerners bear little resemblance to those Jacobs describes in *Incidents* or that one encounters in other antebellum slavery narratives, and certainly not in the British-originated *History of Mary Prince*, not in Hannah Crafts's *The Bondwoman's Narrative*, nor in Harriet E. Wilson's North-based *Our Nig*, for that matter.[3] As Lucky establishes, Riley illustrates a deep and complex relationship with the white women who owned her and her own (also enslaved) black women kin; those bonds, Riley asserts, lacked the peculiar horrors that typified most owner-chattel relations in the antebellum Carolinas. Moreover, Riley claims that she enjoyed extraordinary protection and freedom while still enslaved and that she later enjoyed the privileges of a married woman despite having left her husband. Conversely, as Lucky outlines, there is fascinating resonance between Riley's and Jacobs's respective accounts of relationships among and between women, across racial as well as geopolitical lines, before the Civil War and after. Furthermore, counter to the cast of pseudonymously named characters populating *Incidents*, Riley discusses none of her siblings at length. That is to cite just two of the dramatic ways these compellingly and beautifully written autobiographies both resist and affirm one another. In other words, Riley's *Mysterious Life and Calling* shifts and revises what we thought we knew about black (women's) autobiography, antebellum autobiography, spiritual and conversion texts, slavery narratives, and South Carolina history.

A Mysterious Life and Calling fits equally well into another thrilling and momentous tradition currently garnering overdue attention: black print culture studies. Riley's text takes on added importance given its original publication in 1902 by Daniel Joseph Jenkins, a respected black pastor and entrepreneur as well as the founder of the Jenkins Orphanage Institute in Riley's native Charleston, and more significantly, the owner of a printing press and publisher of regional African American authors and local black newspapers. Lucky's edition of Riley's narrative extends the academic, scholastic, intellectual, and cultural contexts we need to continue examining as we seek to uncover and understand nineteenth-century African American print culture (and) media and their usages. Similarly, Riley's uses narrative deployment of black print culture artifacts—embedded documents sent or given to her and also newspaper clippings, quite literally. Another brilliant aspect of *A Mysterious Life and Calling* is Riley's (putatively uncensored) inclusion of many letters she received: a familiar trope of especial significance within African American life-writing traditions. This tradition in nineteenth-century black (women's) literary studies can be seen in related recovery projects such as Farah Griffin's 2001 edition of the midcentury personal letters exchanged by Addie Brown and Rebecca Primus, in a volume titled *Beloved Sisters and Loving Friends*.

Furthermore, Lucky's edition resonates with several volumes in the Schomburg Library of Nineteenth-Century Black Women Writers (e.g., Anthony Barthelemy's *Collected Black Women's Narratives*, which includes the Christian exhorter and missionary story in *A Narrative of the Life and Travels of Mrs. Nancy Prince*). *A Nickel and a Prayer*, written by Jane Edna Hunter in 1941 (and edited by Rhondda R. Thomas in 2011), is another recently reissued Carolina autobiography that Riley's book complements. Finally, readers would benefit from immersion into Lucky's introduction together with Rhondda Robinson Thomas and Susan Ashton's acclaimed *The South Carolina Roots of African American Thought: A Reader*, which contains excerpts from speeches, correspondence, and life writings from Daniel Payne and Martin Delany of the nineteenth century to Eugene Robinson and Armstrong Williams of twentieth-century South Carolina. Lucky has meticulously documented Riley's birth environs and definitively identified many of the more than 150 people referenced (by name and anonymously) in *A Mysterious Life and Calling*, Payne included.

The increased publication of African American women's writings on multiple fronts formed a principal reason for new and renewed attention to women's contributions to US black life and literature. As many scholars have remarked, 1970s black protofeminist movements emerging out of social progress movements of the 1950s and '60s increased not only the numbers of African American students enrolled in college courses but also the numbers of African Americans included on syllabi for courses in black studies, women's studies, and later black women's studies—both disparate and overlapping disciplines committed to getting works from Maya Angelou's *I Know Why the Caged Bird Sings* (1970) and Toni Morrison's *The Bluest Eye* (1970) to Harriet E. Wilson's *Our Nig* (1859) and Frances E. W. Harper's *Iola Leroy* (1892) in students' hands and keeping them in print and on shelves.[4] Devoted activists and educators—Riley's professional and cultural progeny—have ensured a rightful place for *A Mysterious Life and Calling* in twenty-first-century life: in the academy, in the church hall, and beyond. In sum, *A Mysterious Life and Calling* emerges into a thrilling range of texts representing African American literature, culture, history, historiography, truths, and triumphs. The contribution it stands to make to current conversations is immeasurable. How lucky we all are.

Notes

1.   Thank you to Rhondda R. Thomas, who alerted me to *The Colored Lady Evangelist: Being the Life, Labors, and Experiences of Mrs. Harriet A. Baker* (1892).

2.   Some persons contend this distinction falls to *The Bondwoman's Narrative*, by Hannah Crafts.

3.   Rhondda R. Thomas referred me to a forthcoming biography by Gregg Hecimovich tentatively titled *The Life and Times of Hannah Crafts*.

4.   Each of these works has been republished since their original appearance. For the most recent editions, see the bibliography.

ACKNOWLEDGMENTS

In 2003, I visited the archives of the Stokes Library at the historically black Wilberforce University in Ohio. The rooms dedicated to the historical records of the African Methodist Episcopal (AME) Church, the university, and various aspects of African American life and culture are packed from front to back. Boxes full of donated collections litter the floor. Records of church proceedings line the stacks. Photographs of persistent and serious-looking students and faculty adorn the walls. The place begs exploration and procrastination.

I was there to research AME church records and conference proceedings. One afternoon, I remembered a conversation with my history department colleague. He was doubtful there existed a Southern counterpart to the nineteenth-century freeborn black preaching women of the North who had recounted their stories in autobiographical form. The possibility intrigued me, so I scoured the shelves in search of such a text. When I uncovered the autobiography of Charlotte Riley, a nineteenth-century black preaching woman from Charleston, South Carolina, I was astonished. Mrs. Jacqueline Brown, one of Wilberforce's brilliant and tireless librarians (along with Ms. Dorothy Ayers), shared my joy in becoming acquainted with a black woman who was born into South Carolina slavery but managed to have a quite distinctive career as a schoolteacher, preacher in the South Carolina Conference of the AME Church, and public servant in post–Civil War South Carolina.

The reissuing of this important text would not have been possible without the support and guidance of several individuals and institutions. I am grateful to my home institution, Villanova University, for generous funding from both a Christian R. and Mary F. Lindback Foundation Minority Junior Faculty Award and a Ford Foundation postdoctoral fellowship. Mrs. Brown will forever be in my debt, not only for her kindness and boundless knowledge, but also for her unwavering dedication to the Stokes Library and the Wilberforce University community. Her commitment harkens back to an earlier time. During my visits to South Carolina, I made many friends: the librarians and archivists at the Charleston County Public Library, South Carolina Library, and both Georgette Mayo and Harlan Greene of the Avery Research Center for African American History and Culture. The center is a precious jewel, the "Schomburg of the South." In keeping with Riley's theme of the "mysterious," I experienced my own mystery in the form of Samad Hadis, a kind library patron who inquired one day about my research at the Charleston Public Library, disappeared, and then reappeared with four copies of the February 22, 2003, edition of the *Post and Courier*, which featured a front-page article on Lincolnville's Jubilee celebration, replete with color photographs of Riley's church, Ebenezer AME, and Bishop Richard Harvey Cain, the town's founder. Then he disappeared for good. Thank you. I was also privileged to meet and befriend Christine Hampton, resident Lincolnville expert and coauthor (with her sister, Rosalee W. Washington) of *The History of Lincolnville, South Carolina*. I cannot thank her, her husband, James C. Hampton, or my fellow elder in the Church of the Living God International, Inc., Pastor Cornelius Hudson, enough for trudging through the overgrown weeds and brambles of the Bible Sojourner Cemetery in search of Riley's grave. I felt like Alice Walker in search of Zora Neale Hurston. My ever-changing research assistants were so helpful—Katherine Harris, Nicole Saitta, Liv McMullen, Jessica Lasak, Rebecca Buckham, Cynthia Estremera, Joseph Landgraf, and Anna Fitzpatrick. So important to this project has been William Andrews, the series editor. From the beginning, he encouraged me that I had unearthed a "find" and waited patiently for me while I juggled my overextended preaching, teaching, and administrative schedule. He is a true friend and gentleman in every sense of the word.

Finally, to my Sword of the Spirit and Church of the Living God International Church families; my parents, Arvelle and Esther Jones; and my son and husband, Caleb and Timmy, thank you for your love and support.

A Mysterious Life and Calling

Introduction

One evening in the early 1880s, Charlotte Riley heard a knock at the door of her pretty, little home in the Negro village of Lincolnville, South Carolina. The all-black, incorporated town founded by AME Bishop Richard Cain had been in existence only a little over a decade and was home to African Americans recently delivered from the physical and emotional torture of American slavery. Riley and her assistant, Anna Simonds, with whom she lived and relied upon like an older mother would her daughter, never locked the door to their frequent visitors, both black and white. They were at home preparing their guest room to host Bishop John Brown, who had come to preach at St. Peter's AME Church. So when the knocking continued after Riley said, "Come" repeatedly, she called out sternly, "Why not come in?" As she approached the door, it opened and a tall white man entered her home. Intimidated by his height, broad hat, and large pipe, she remained calm and invited the visitor to be seated but intuitively knew that she needed to protect herself. While Lincolnville was quaint and safe, black people were being attacked all over the South in the aftermath of Reconstruction. Lynchings were common, and white hatred of black economic progress was thinly veiled after the Betrayal of 1877.[1] So she left Anna sitting with the stranger, went into her bedroom, retrieved her revolver, cocked it, put it in her pocket, signaled her neighbor from her bedroom window that she might be in trouble, and "got ready for battle." The stranger indicated that he had heard that the people who ran the local school were named Simonds and told Riley that his brother had a "colored family in Charleston." The man, who never offered his first name, had come to see if they were the right people since his last name was also Simonds. When Riley assured him that both Anna's and her father were black, Mr. Simonds assured the women that he was a gentleman and that they had no need to fear. Riley

had no fear in chastising him for coming into her home wearing a hat and
smoking a pipe: "Sir," she said, "you ought to have proven that as you entered
the door. I am not alarmed but for your rude act. The most common man
around here would not do it." Although he apologized and removed the hat
and pipe, Riley's earlier signal had alerted the men of the community, including
the marshal. They burst into the house shouting, "Halt!" and removed the
intruder to question him. He left telling the town's men the same story he had
given Riley. Later, word got back to Riley that, in fact, the man was wanted for
the murder of his wife. "The rumor ran high the next day over the town that
our teacher silenced the revolver of the bushwhacker"; Riley, instead, attributed
her protection to "God's mysterious power," the same mysterious power that
had emancipated her from slavery, called her to the preaching ministry, pulled
her into public service, protected her from dangers seen and unseen, and
moved her to write. The result, *The Autobiography: A Mysterious Life and Calling by
the Noted and Famous Rev. Mrs. C. S. Riley of Lincolnville, S. C.*, offers a unique
glimpse into the life of a black preaching woman who was both born into South
Carolina slavery and ministered officially within the auspices of the African
Methodist Episcopal (AME) Church south of the Mason-Dixon Line. Donated
to Wilberforce University as a part of the Levi Jenkins Coppin Collection,[2] the
only extant copy of *The Autobiography: A Mysterious Life and Calling* had fallen out
of circulation: until now, it has neither been registered with the Library of
Congress nor published in any contemporary critical edition. Published inde-
pendently around 1902 by the Industrial Department of the Daniel Jenkins
Orphanage,[3] Riley's one-hundred-page narrative is the first of its kind.[4]

The text presents few but nevertheless important details about Charlotte
Riley's childhood and young adult life in slavery. She experienced an unusual
form of bondage, one that allowed her to gain a quasi-formal education, inte-
grate socially with prominent white South Carolinians, and participate in a
formal marriage ceremony to a free black man, all while she was still a slave.
The narrative also tells of Riley's conversion to Christianity and provides a
detailed accounting of the development of her formal relationship with the AME
Church as an institution and with its male preachers, presiding elders, and at
least ten bishops, most of whom showed her great support. Her text functions
as a necessary chapter in AME Church history, an additional and critical primary source by which to investigate the workings of the most influential black
religious institution of the nineteenth century. Charlotte Riley's work with the
AME Church was extensive. Through it, she developed into a seasoned teacher,
helped to establish schools, and contributed to the building of churches in South
Carolina and the spread of the Christian gospel to many in the area: blacks and

whites, men and women. One preacher noted that she was the only woman preacher in the state of South Carolina, likely referring to her status as a formally licensed minister, which was rarely achieved at that time among black or white preaching women. Finally, Riley served an important role as a civil servant after the Civil War and into the beginning of the twentieth century, assisting black men and women in their struggle to create for themselves meaningful lives in a country violently conflicted about its black citizenry. *A Mysterious Life and Calling* reacquaints contemporary readers both with the complex world of Southern slavery, specifically as it was practiced in and around Charleston, South Carolina, and with black women who worked to enter the formal ranks of the preaching ministry. The text borrows from both the fugitive slave narrative and the black-preaching-women's narrative forms, thus complicating readers' understanding of the lived experiences of antebellum and post–Civil War black Americans.

——

Like formerly enslaved black writers and black preaching women who un-folded their life stories in narrative form, Charlotte S. Riley begins her autobiog-raphy by explaining her decision to write. Employing both the words of the biblical Psalms and the Enlightenment philosopher, Voltaire, she expresses her desire to help "some young, ambitious, yet fearful heart" who might "arise and ascend the hill of difficulty and reflect the honor of his maker." Her use of the third-person masculine pronoun "his" indicates that she is thinking not just of young women who might follow her example either in the work of the ministry or of social uplift, but also of all those who, inspired by reading about her life, would seek to better their spiritual, economic, and political conditions. More-over, she chooses to write not from a place of vanity and pride, but rather to accommodate the request of her "many admiring friends of all classes." Like her fugitive and preaching forerunners—Jarena Lee, Frederick Douglass, Henry "Box" Brown, Solomon Northup, Harriet Jacobs, and Julia Foote—it appears she joined the writerly community reluctantly but fully aware of the weight of her choice. While she was never a fugitive, choosing to remain with her mistress through her teenage years and young adulthood, her autobiography shares characteristics with the fugitive slave narrative form. She offers specific details about her birth, family, and early life and describes the unique conditions of her enslavement. She even provides the names of slaveholding whites with whom she appears to have had congenial relationships. Alongside the details of her preaching and civil activities, she comments on the institution of slavery, the aftermath of Reconstruction, and the perilous years that followed. For students of the slave narrative, Riley's musings on her early life as a slave in Charleston offer insight into the nuanced and complicated workings of urban slavery during the nineteenth century.

Born a slave in Charleston, South Carolina, on August 26, 1839, the only daughter of enslaved parents, John and Sarah Levy, the young Charlotte grew up under somewhat idyllic circumstances. The Levys raised their daughter and four sons in the major seaport city of Charleston, whose coastal setting offered a range of opportunities for members of both the free and enslaved black communities to live more "normal" lives in terms of housing, employment, religious expression, and mobility than their rural counterparts, who found themselves isolated on plantations of various sizes. Although historians have well documented the vagaries of urban slavery, the city also offered a space within which some slave families could function as somewhat stable units.[5] Although poor and enslaved, the Levys were allowed to hire out their time at $5 to $10 per month and to rent a private room in town away from their master; they were also permitted to keep their children to themselves until they were grown to what Riley calls "years of usefulness." Such was the case for many enslaved blacks in Charleston, who were used, according to the historian Bernard E. Powers Jr., in various unskilled and semiskilled capacities as engineers, carpenters, blacksmiths, coopers, bricklayers, shipbuilders, steamboat hands and pilots, leather craftsmen, firemen, domestics, and mechanics.[6] Additionally, while strict South Carolina law forbad the teaching of slaves to read and write, the city of Charleston had a history of allowing free blacks to establish schools to educate their children to aid in their professional training and to learn the Bible. "Urban life provided many informal means for slaves to acquire a knowledge of reading and writing, and some even managed to attend clandestine schools."[7] Thus the coastal, southern city allowed black people possibilities to give their lives meaning and to resist the debilitating effects of slavery.

Displaying a "superior spirit" as a child, Riley loved books and letters beyond her age, more so than her siblings, none of whom are named in her text. The children were permitted to attend one such trade school, run by a local widow, to learn a skill that would make them profitable to their owners. Young Charlotte received a remarkable education in sewing, math, reading, and classical literature. Her school attendance nevertheless seems to have been hindered by her poor health, because she was "born a slave to disease, having inherited nervous headache: . . . not . . . so far away from the point to call it disease of the brain."[8] Suffering from what appears to have been debilitating migraines, Riley was plagued her entire life. The condition caused her to move slowly and to avoid excitement, except in the case of ministry, where she admits to preaching vigorously and making alarming appeals "for the unsaved to accept the terms of the 'glorious Gospel of God's only Son' that aroused the meeting to a fever heat of the 'Spirit that burns in the soul.'"[9]

Charlotte Riley's early childhood was similar to that of two other black women who were born into slavery but afforded some protection from slavery's harshest conditions and chose to document their lives in writing. The fugitive slave narrator Harriet Jacobs was born in Edenton, North Carolina, in 1813 and published the account of her harrowing experiences, *Incidents in the Life of a Slave Girl Written by Herself*, in 1861. Like Riley, Jacobs learned to read and write when she was a child, by the permission of her first mistress. Her mother and father were allowed to live in their own home in the coastal city of Edenton, which, like Charleston, offered a space within which young Harriet could be initially sheltered from the unwelcomed intrusions of her later owners. She writes,

> My father was a carpenter, and considered so intelligent and skillful in his trade, that, when buildings out of the common line were to be erected, he was sent for from long distances to be head workman. On condition of paying his mistress two hundred dollars a year, and supporting himself, he was allowed to work at his trade, and manage his own affairs. His strongest wish was to purchase his children; but, though he several times offered his hard earnings for that purpose, he never succeeded. . . . They lived together in a comfortable home; and, though we were all slaves, I was so fondly shielded that I never dreamed I was a piece of merchandise, trusted to them for safe keeping, and liable to be demanded of them at any moment.[10]

Both Jacobs and Riley lived as children relatively unaware of the brutalities associated with the slave system: the forced separation of families, the pain of the lash, physical deprivation, and starvation. However, when Jacobs's first mistress died in 1825, her life changed dramatically. As she grew into the dreaded "years of usefulness," Jacobs became the property of Mary Matilda Norcom, who was initially too young to serve as her mistress. So, as Jacobs entered puberty and young womanhood, she became subject to the psychic and sexual violation that resulted from the father's, Dr. James Norcom's, mercurial temper and lascivious behavior. Such was not the case for Riley. Though her father lived until she was twenty-two, her mother died when she was too young to remember. She had an uncle and at least one grandmother who helped to raise her. Eventually, she began to live with her grandmother's mistress, Mrs. John Wilkes, an older woman who had no children. She took Charlotte "at an early age to her use and care," thus sparing her a life of fear and sexual vulnerability. Riley was given extraordinary liberty in her social interactions and allowed to be quite mobile with limited supervision. Although Riley writes little of her daily life in bondage, she does note that she "had so much spirit of freedom instilled in me that it was no easy matter to try to subdue it. My inner nature resented any attempt at oppression, so I grew up with a will to do the right and fear no evil."[11]

Likewise, Susie King Taylor describes receiving similar support in her autobiographical narrative, *Reminiscences of My Life in Camp with the 33d United States Colored Troops Late 1st South Carolina Volunteers*, first published in 1902. Born Susie Baker in 1848, Riley's contemporary was born a slave in Savannah, Georgia, and was also reared under the protective care of her grandmother, who governed her own home and sent her young granddaughter to school in the home of her widowed friend. Taylor's narrative, which includes attestations by the noted military officers Col. Thomas Wentworth Higginson and Col. C. T. Trowbridge, highlights her family's ancestry, which includes a great-great-grandmother who lived to be 120 years old and a great-grandmother who lived to be 100. The matrilineal strength Susie King Taylor gained from these women, along with the presence of her mother and father, gave her the succor she needed to undertake her groundbreaking work as a Civil War nurse and educator.[12]

During the Civil War, Mrs. Wilkes took Charlotte Riley to Anderson County, South Carolina, about 200 miles northwest of Charleston, to remain there until the end of the conflict because the coastal city was under siege. During her stay, she was approached by the town architect, a free black man named Cornelius Riley. Anderson, like Charleston, could boast of a diversified black work force that consisted of both enslaved and free blacks. By 1850, "almost 82 percent of all free black workers were engaged in either skilled or semiskilled occupations," and by 1860, free black men were employed in more than sixty different occupations as carpenters, painters, tailors, brick masons, and, in far less numbers, shipping clerks, bookkeepers, and entrepreneurs.[13] As an architect, Cornelius Riley would have been a rare but conceivable entity. When he expressed his interest in her, however, Charlotte rebuffed his advances and explained that she had no intention of leaving her mistress. Cornelius Riley promised to "wait on time to settle the matter." In a surprising turn of events, Wilkes died in less than fifteen days, which allowed the slave woman to accept Riley's marriage proposal. Coincidentally, her grandmother also died while she was away. In one of the most telling passages of the text, Charlotte lists the names of the white South Carolina families who were present at her August 25, 1864, wedding, who included Captain William Henry Perrenneu, one of the most prominent South Carolinians of the time, in whose parlor Riley's nuptials took place. In one sense, she seems to take the relationships for granted since she was raised "under the direction of the most intelligent class of persons . . . and emulated their nature and refinement."[14] Yet she notes that her "colored friends were accorded a place among them, only less in number, but all was as kind as friends could be, with no exceptions. Even their owners were very indulgent in every way and manner."[15]

Charlotte Riley's experiences with upper-class slaveholding families helped to shape her life in profound ways. They offered her protection from sexual abuse and other forms of harsh physical treatment, a comfortable living environment, adequate food and clothing, access to superior education, and, it appears, human kindness. It is important to note, however, that while she characterizes her relationships as amicable, they must be read through the veil and influence of an institution that resisted human freedom and legally disallowed formal education for enslaved black people. The list of the names of well-known slaveholding families should be read, in part, as an indictment of the institution. Forty years after emancipation, Riley provides a formal roll call of those who participated in the country's most shameful project.

Moreover, Riley's reference to Sullivan's Island as the site of her conversion complicates her narrative ordering of events. Located southeast of Charleston and termed "the Ellis Island of black Americans," from 1700 to the end of the colonial period Sullivan's Island served as a gateway to slavery in America for tens of thousands of captured Africans. Between 1700 and 1800, at the height of the Atlantic slave trade, approximately 40 percent of Africans who were forcibly shipped to mainland North America came to the shores of South Carolina. Approximately one hundred thousand African immigrants came through Charleston harbor and were first quarantined on the island in buildings called pest houses, similar to structures that would later be used on New York's Ellis Island, to rid them of diseases they may have contracted during the Middle Passage. The island, no doubt, held a special place in Riley's memory as a treasured location for relaxation; however, in the collective memory of American slaves, particularly South Carolinians, Sullivan's Island loomed as a place of quarantine and isolation. In the narrative, it serves as a symbol of both spiritual freedom and physical bondage.[16]

Finally, it should also be noted that although Riley outlines her wartime activities and movement away from Charleston in 1864, neither she nor Susie King Taylor devotes any space in their texts to their experience with freedom. Readers are left to assume that Riley was freed as a result of the war and the death of her mistress. She indicates that she wrote a song about Emancipation

Map of Charleston Harbor

Day, which she sang at the dedication of the historic Emanuel AME Church and years later during President Theodore Roosevelt's train stop through Lincolnville. Yet she is oddly silent about her personal experience with emancipation from bondage. Fugitive slave narrators, like Frederick Douglass and Harriet Jacobs, were careful not to reveal the full details of their escape routes in the 1840s and 1850s, lest they spoil the chances of their fellow enslaved brothers and sisters who might try to similarly emancipate themselves. However, writers of the fugitive slave narrative always described the sweet taste of freedom. For Riley, who remained in her native South Carolina, freedom served as a means to an end and not the end itself. Riley's decision not to express her feelings outright point to the primary aim of her work: emancipation afforded both Riley and Taylor the opportunity to serve their people without limitation. And for Riley, who would spend at least the next forty years in Christian ministry, freedom from the sin of slavery allowed her the freedom to preach against the slavery of sin.

———

In 1853, at the age of fourteen, Riley was permitted to visit her friend Myra Rivers on Sullivan's Island, about ten miles from downtown Charleston. Riley had been raised as a Presbyterian, but while she was visiting her friend, the two attended "an old time Methodist watch-night meeting." While there, Riley questioned her friend about the necessity of "shouting" at the meeting, a physical manifestation of the Holy Spirit in which worshippers either move in a group in a circular fashion or individually in ecstatic demonstration. Common to early Methodist worship, the practice was not characteristic of the Presbyterian Church and would have likely been unfamiliar to and uncomfortable for Riley. She retired for the evening and had a vision. In it, a man came to Riley's bedside and spoke to her "with an authority to be obeyed," placing him in the category of an angel or Christ-figure. He led her "through a beautiful passage up to a beautiful building, into a spacious room" where she heard people singing inspiriting songs. The gentleman invited her to join in the singing and shouting, but Riley refused. He joined in, and before long, Riley did as well. She was so caught up in the activity that she was among the last to be taken away from the assembly. The man led her back "through the moonlight" to her room and requested that she meet him in three weeks at another meeting; he also challenged her not to allow anything or anyone to keep her from attending. Taking literal the instructions she received in the vision, three weeks later and after overcoming obstacles of bad weather and unreliable transportation, Riley attended the meeting, was touched by the Holy Spirit, and fell away in a swoon for three days.

Riley's description of her conversion experience places her narrative squarely within a literary tradition established by African American preaching women of the nineteenth century: the black preaching woman's narrative. Beginning with Maria Stewart's public addresses in 1831 in Boston and the publication of Jarena Lee's slim autobiographical volume in 1836, black preaching women have outlined their lived experiences in public service and their attempts to gain access to the formal ranks of ministry and church leadership. The works of Stewart, Lee, Zilpha Elaw, Julia Foote, and Amanda Berry Smith, among others, introduced readers and scholars to black women who felt called to preach a Christian gospel and work in ministry but who did so with little or no religious institutional support or sanction. The women wrote of their lives and work throughout the nineteenth century and into the next but were all born free in the North and never lived directly under the horrors of American chattel slavery in the South. With the exception of Stewart, their ministries were centered in the mid-Atlantic states and extended only for short stints into the South or, for one woman, to Europe.[17] The narratives share characteristics of the Protestant spiritual narrative in that they demonstrate the narrator's quest for spiritual perfection in an imperfect world, witness the writer's conversion in an effort to influence an unredeemed readership, and record her trials, temptations, and final triumph. Black preaching women's spiritual narratives accomplish these narrative tasks and extend beyond the experiential emphasis of white men to include the spiritual experiences of black women who feel themselves called to preach the gospel and endeavor to enter formal ministry. Characterized by several salient features, black preaching women's spiritual narratives call both a black and white readership to moral reform and for male church leadership to recognize the validity of women's evangelical ministry. The narratives rehearse the narrator's early life experiences, moment of conversion, subsequent call to preach, and ministerial activities. Additionally, the women reveal their struggles with self-doubt and their ongoing conflicts with spouses who either die or eventually disappear. While Charlotte Riley's text appears to be a straightforward, linear accounting of these critical moments, it highlights her extraordinary preaching career, her official appointments to the ranks of church leadership, and the fact that she received formal church licensure by the AME Church to preach.

One of the distinctive narrative features of Riley's text is her repeated reliance on the mysterious, which is invoked first in the title, *A Mysterious Life and Calling*. In one sense, this characteristic privileges the spiritual over her physical concerns as a slave or as a woman hindered by poor health, for it focuses her motives for writing in terms of a divine "calling." Like other black women spiritual narrators, Riley attributes her decision to write her autobiography not from selfish or self-centered motives, but rather to "comply with the request of my many admiring friends of all classes, believing as they have so urgently told me that the work will be an incentive to some young ambitious, yet fearful heart." This was true of Zilpha Elaw, for example, who in 1846 desired after her five-year evangelical stay in London to leave a parting gift to her friends and colleagues that might encourage them to live a pious and holy life. At the end of the century, Amanda Smith wrote in response to her many friends who urged her to write "an account of [her] life, and let it be known how *God has led you out into His work*."[18] Riley's apologia leaves any potential criticism of herself as a writer in "the hands of those who constrained me to make this attempt at writing up my life so full of mystery, (Amen)." The shroud of mystery and her dependence on others for affirmation to write provides protection for Riley and other black women spiritual writers from systematic criticism for entering the male-dominated realm of preaching and ministry. The combination of mystery and self-effacement is powerful. If Riley is criticized, even for referring to herself as both "noted and famous," she can say that her friends and admirers have told her to undertake the work, not that she has undertaken the work from vanity or pride. To support the entire ministerial endeavor, she relies on the mysteries of God and on the unknowable, unquantifiable realm of the Spirit. The shroud of "the mysterious" serves in the narrative as a sign for authority and right. Riley circles back to the mysterious as she recounts significant events in her life, such as her conversion to Christianity, commitment to teaching, transactions in business, or protection from danger, in an effort to prove that her life, calling, and ministry are covered in mystery and sanctioned by the divine.

Equally important, nineteenth-century black preaching women's narratives describe the women's conversion experiences using similar imagery and include a recognition of the narrator's sinful state and need for salvation, a dramatic and life-altering encounter with God, doubtfulness as to whether the transformation will last, and an ultimate confirmation of its completion. For example, born in 1790, Zilpha Elaw was reared in Pennsylvania by religious parents. After the deaths of her mother and father, the unconverted Elaw was convicted of her sinfulness by her youthful actions, perceived herself as sinful, and was affected often by prophetic nightmares. After waking from one such dream, Elaw was terrified and moved to tears upon realizing her sinful condition. That morning, she writes, she shared her experience with the woman for whom she worked, who tried to convince the young Elaw to forget her dreams; however, Elaw asserts that "she failed in her attempt to tranquilize my mind, because the convictions of my sinfulness in the sight of God, and incompetency to meet my Judge, were immovable and distressing. I now gave myself much to meditation, and lisped out my simple and feeble prayers to God, as well as my limited apprehensions and youthful abilities admitted."[19] Elaw privileged her own intuitive knowledge over supposed white authority when her employer attempted to divert her attention away from spirituality by taking away her Bible. Despite Elaw's social status as a discountable servant, she was strengthened by her own grasp of reality. She then went to hear the Methodists preach, and although she had been trained in the Quaker tradition, she was convinced of the verity of Methodist doctrine.[20]

A similar experience was that of Rebecca Cox Jackson, who was born at the end of the eighteenth century and was a charismatic itinerant preacher who founded a Shaker religious community in Philadelphia. In July 1830, Jackson was awakened by a thunderstorm. Fearful, she paced the floor wringing her hands and heard a voice inform her, "This day thy soul is required of thee."[21] Her fear caused her to kneel in prayer. She writes that the more she prayed the worse she felt, and although "all of [her] sins from [her] childhood rushed into [her] mind like an over swelling tide, she continued praying, 'Lord, I never will rise from my knees till thou for Christ's sake has mercy on my poor sinking soul or sends me to Hell.'"[22] According to Jackson's journal, as a result of this powerful religious experience, she received not only salvation but also the gifts of literacy, healing, and the ability to control the weather.[23]

In each conversion instance, there is a Christ or God figure in the vision or trance who functions as a guiding and protecting parent and often bathes the convert in healing waters. The man in Riley's vision leads her "through a beautiful passage" to the revival meeting and back "through the moonlight" to her room after the singing and shouting. The images are commensurate with those of new birth, where the God/parent figure also acts as midwife, ushering the spiritually reborn into a new life. Moreover, the recurring representations of whiteness, light, and spotless garments, or the lack thereof, point to a duality defined by interiority and exteriority. Sue Houchins has interpreted such images theologically and warns against secularizing them.[24] Carla Peterson argues that references in these narratives to the physical self within a spiritual context are "illustrative of the 'body in pain' that manifested itself during periods of intense spiritual oppression."[25] For black women spiritual narrators, the problem of reconciling the possession of an enlightened and pure, or "whitened," soul within a black and female servant body was always present, illuminating the bind such writers faced.[26] For those narrators who referenced their race and gender in the expanded titles of their narratives, negotiation between their interior and exterior selves required them to reference rebirth and to use images like white garments and light to make a claim that despite their status as devalued black women within the larger social sphere, their experiences were honorable and clean before God.

Besides the intensity of Riley's conversion experience at such a young age and her ability to travel freely while enslaved, Riley's repeated use of the number three is also worth noting. She is to meet the man from the vision three weeks after their initial encounter, which falls on the third Saturday of September, and she swoons for three days, "abiding in a world of love and glory," after her conversion. Combined with the logging of her ministerial travels, Riley's use of the number three, in probable descriptions of actual occurrences, binds her narrative to that which is holy—the Trinity, Christ's entombment, Jonah's entrapment in the whale's belly, the amount of days, weeks, and years of pro-phetic fulfillment—and, like spiritual narrators before her, situates her in the "divine scheme of things." The number is used to denote the passage of time and stands as a figure for the "fullness of time," a reminder that in Riley's scheme of things, "God's time is right and sufficient."[27] Combined with Riley's use of the mysterious, the narrative impact is powerful.

The power of the narrative was always important for women whose physical presence was consistently scrutinized. Such was certainly the case for Riley, who was always aware of her tenuous position in the public sphere; she repeat-edly refers to herself in the narrative as a "woman" preacher. For some, her existence posed problems. She relates an incident in which a white man followed close behind her after hearing her preach, making her uncomfortable, to deter-mine if she were a "*real* woman or an angel." She was proven to be flesh and blood and that her "fur capes were not wings." At another church, a black woman approached her saying, "The white lady I work for told me to 'look at your fingers and see is you a real woman.'"[28] Like Jarena Lee, who was simi-larly accosted, Riley was faced with skepticism from whites and blacks about whether a real woman could be a preacher and, in turn, whether a preacher could really be a woman.

During the course of her adult life, Charlotte Riley came to rely on two women, Mary Speissegger and Anna Simonds, for traveling companionship and succor. Her weakened health precluded her from living alone. These women aided her in traveling, assisted her in ministry, and, in the case of Simonds, took the place of the daughter Riley never had. Although Jarena Lee often traveled alone, her narrative refers to constant fellowship among sisters when she traveled and when she returned home. At least one time, she shared the pulpit with Zilpha Elaw and notes that "we enjoyed good seasons together. . . . I was informed by those that were in the spirit, that they saw the glory of God like a sun over the pulpit, and a face shone after it, thus the battle was the Lord's."[29] Julia Foote became acquainted with three women in Philadelphia with whom she ran an eleven-night revival. Because these preaching women were often alone, outnumbered and outranked by their male counterparts, fellowship among African American women would have been vital.

In teaching, marriage, ministry, public service, business, and physical protec-tion, the cumulative effect of Riley's mysterious encounters bolsters the narrative with "otherworldly" authority that, when juxtaposed with the self-effacement evident in her decision to undertake the narrative project, underscores her power as a preacher. The day that Riley received her local preacher's license, for example, Elder Hiram Young announced that Riley would be bringing the afternoon message. She says that "at the close of my weak yet earnest effort in setting forth the 'Safety of God's people' under so great a defender, so strong a protector, sixteen souls came forward and joined in the army of the 'Lord on the terms of the Gospel.'"[30] The strength of her experience parallels that of the earliest recorded preaching moment by a black woman in an autobiography. When the preacher scheduled for the afternoon's service faltered in his speech and "[lost] the spirit," Jarena Lee jumped to her feet and delivered a powerful exhortation, interrupting the official preacher. Like her Northern counterparts, Riley posits herself as a weak vessel, yet she is protected by a strong God. The result is the garnering for the AME Church of sixteen individuals who expressed an interest in Christian conversion in the wake of her preaching right from the start of her ministerial career. The conclusion to be drawn is clear: Riley functions within the accepted parameters for women in ministry, yet she is vibrant and strong.

Riley's spiritual rebirth catapulted her into a life of service, teaching, and preaching that would continue into the early twentieth century. First, however, she faced the challenge of aligning ministry and marriage. Perhaps because she married so close to the war's end, Riley seems unconcerned about the marriage ceremony's validity or the potential for familial instability due to the erratic sale of family members under the slave system. She does mention that the couple lost their "marriage paper" when they moved to Columbia after the war but notes that they easily obtained a replacement from Bishop John M. Brown of the AME Church. Cornelius Riley could not accept the seriousness with which his wife took her call to preach, causing the couple to quarrel early in their marriage about her commitment to teaching and ministry. She was later isolated when her husband decided to move her to Columbia, away from her church and work in Charleston.

Problems of marriage and motherhood are of paramount importance in black preaching women's narratives. Whether enslaved or free, the preaching women are concerned about whether their marital relationships will interfere with their ecclesiastical duties. Several times, for example, Jarena Lee mentions her sick son, whom she leaves with friends after the death of her husband in order to take preaching engagements miles from her home. The same is true for Zilpha Elaw, whose daughter encouraged her to go and preach "and do not think any thing about me, for I shall do very well."[31] In each case, the women were married to uncooperative husbands, some of whom left the women conveniently widowed; all of whom were seen as a hindrance to the women's ministries. Julia Foote says of her husband that he said, "I was getting more crazy every day, and getting others in the same way, and that if I did not stop he would send me back home or to the crazy-house."[32]

Amanda Berry Smith's situation is quite interesting. She chose to remarry after the death of her first husband, Calvin Devine, whom she had married in 1854 at the age of seventeen. Several years after Devine's death in the Civil War, the widowed Amanda met and married her second husband, James Smith, an ordained deacon in the AME Church, who was thus qualified to preach locally. He was also twenty years her senior and had an eighteen-year-old daughter of his own. It seems that Smith remarried primarily for two reasons. The first, although not explicitly stated, was to provide an economically stable environment for her then nine-year-old daughter, Maize. She writes, "During the years of my widowhood I boarded my little girl, here a while and then there. Sometimes she was well taken care of and at other times was not; for I found that often people do things just for the little money they get out of it; and when I would go and see the condition of my poor child, and then had to turn away and leave her and go to my work I often cried and prayed; but what could I do more?"[33] At this time, Smith had moved to Philadelphia from her home in Lancaster, Pennsylvania. Her anguish over having to leave her child in the charge of people who did not genuinely or even sufficiently care for her is heartwrenching and is indicative of the plight of many free and Northern antebellum black women. Her question, "but what could I do more?" reflects the limited economic and employment possibilities for black women, who most often worked as domestics in white households, as laundresses who took washing into their own substandard dwellings, or in very few cases, as dressmakers or gourmet cooks.[34] For Smith, marriage would have provided her child with a "Christian home" and herself with protection from financial peril and the dangers of being single.

Smith's sanctification and actual preaching ministry did not occur until after her marriage to Smith, but she had begun to desire to work in the capacity of an evangelist and had told her husband so before their marriage. "He quite agreed to it all," she writes, "and told me he was preparing himself to join the Conference and so go into the itinerant work."[35] She writes clearly that her reason for marrying was to carve out an acceptable space within which she could pursue her burgeoning interests in church work and the enactment of Christian compassion. Although I would not argue that Smith was as aware of the "marriage tradition in literature and her own subversion of that tradition," as Ann duCille argues was the case in Jacobs's narrative, it is clear to me that

Smith understood the importance of the institution of marriage and attempted
to utilize the "convention of coupling" to subvert gendered church hierarchies,
as duCille conceives of in *The Coupling Convention: Sex, Text, and Tradition in Black
Women's Fiction*.[36] In Amanda's willingness to "learn to love" Smith, in her understanding of how much influence a minister's wife could exert over her husband's
work, and in her admiration for the local preacher and his wife and their team-
like endeavors, Smith clearly "theorized [a] utopian union" in which she was
an "empowered black heroine" who could "achieve parity" with the man she
chose to marry and could "actively participate in the public sphere," through
church work.[37] Unfortunately, James Smith never followed through on his
promises and was as uncommitted to her vision as all the other narrators' husbands proved to be. Ultimately, his death in 1869 of stomach cancer freed
Smith to pursue her spiritual goals, which she began in the same month as his
death. "Since then," she reports confidently, "I have been a widow and have
traveled half way round the world, and God has ever been faithful," pointing to
her husband's unfaithfulness in keeping his earthly promises and God's thorough
sufficiency as a mate.[38]

The Rileys' inability to reconcile Charlotte's need to teach and serve and
Cornelius's dislike of the African Methodists, which Charlotte joined unofficially
after their marriage, caused an irresolvable rift in their marriage. Charlotte
challenged her husband: "Now, you let me alone, and if I am wrong, I shall fail
in the work, but get out of my way, as I am convicted to be right. As a 'child of
God,' He shall guide me, always in the right. This he could not deny, as he had
seen so much of 'God's favor toward me.' So he gave up the battle with never
to come to see me as to intimidate. So the battle is fought, the victory won, and
Zion's field is mine."[39] It seems that Cornelius made good on his threat never
to come see her, for from that point in the narrative, Charlotte never mentions
her husband again.

———

Charlotte Riley appears to have taken both her husband's threat of abandonment and the reality of it in stride, for despite her poor health, she worked tirelessly for over thirty years as a teacher, licensed preacher, missionary, fundraiser,
and political activist in the South Carolina Conference of the AME Church.
Throughout her narrative, she freely intertwines the details of her ministerial
labors with those of her teaching activities and missionary fundraising efforts.
She first taught at a private school run by the Presbyterians, but later the leaders
of the South Carolina Conference recruited her to teach in their school in

Lewisville, which opened in 1866 with seventy-five children. She taught those seventy-five children during the day, twenty-five adult men and women at night, and three hundred children and adults in the Sabbath School with only one additional teacher for three years without a vacation and little pay. At the end of the three years, Riley recounted a second "mysterious" vision.

In the vision, a "person" hands her a letter written in Hebrew, which she cannot interpret. The "spirit being," whose gender she is careful not to identify, calls her "Figrine" and tells her that her mother has sent her a letter from heaven, which she can then supernaturally read: "Be ye truthful, and you shall have a legacy."[40] After the vision, three strangers visited the principal of the Lewisville school to discuss it becoming state funded. The news was quite positive, for such status would ensure that the state of South Carolina would become responsible for paying Riley's salary. The strangers informed her that she would be paid three years' back salary, five cents per day per child. Until that point, Riley's salary was to be paid by the parents, most of whom were newly emancipated black men and women unable to afford to do so. The visitors instructed Riley to submit a report documenting the names of the students, their days' attendance, their parents' names, their addresses, and why their parents had not paid. They also instructed her to file the report with the Legislature at Columbia, the state capital, signed by the School Commissioner and the senator of the county of Orangeburg, South Carolina. At the completion of the process, Riley received a check for $1,300, a legacy, defined in part as "a particular thing or certain sum of money given by the last will or testament. Anything handed down by an ancestor or predecessor." Because the letter supposedly came from her mother from heaven, Riley pauses in the text to pay homage to her mother's memory.

Charlotte Riley rose quickly in the ranks of the AME Church, first becoming a class leader shortly after joining the church organization and then receiving her local preacher's license in 1871.[41] Unlike her Northern, freeborn preaching sisters, such as Jarena Lee, Zilpha Elaw, and Julia Foote, Riley was careful to comment on not only the importance of the spiritual in her life but also on the gendered, racial, and political complexities of working in the AME Church in the South. On the one hand, Riley enjoyed a powerful ministry. On at least one occasion, "the people became unmanageable in the demonstration of the Spirit of love, that the elder and your sister were in danger of being pressed to injury."[42] At another service, more than three thousand people came to hear her preach, both blacks and whites. Attendees always responded positively to her call for salvation at the end of her sermons, and many joined the AME Church as a result of her appeals. On at least one occasion, she preached in

New York in the late 1870s, and although it appears that she never got the opportunity to fulfill the duty, most notable was her appointment as pastor of the Chester Mission AME Church in Columbia, South Carolina, in 1884. It appears that another preacher actually served in the post. For some, her presence in the pulpit was empowering: "The sisters shouted for joy at the reality of my presence. . . . So the multitude was attracted, and seemed to enjoy the very presence of the woman that was to preach on Sunday. They seemed to regard her as a monument of God's mysterious work."[43] The preaching men were "all very kind in their treatment toward me and some of them said they were very proud of the only girl child in the ministerial family, and were proud at any time to have me in their pulpit and under their care."[44] Her position as "the only girl child" and "under the care" of the men might be read as patronizing and demeaning; however, it is clear that her male colleagues welcomed her presence in their churches and pulpits and considered her a member of the ministerial family. Because all of the leadership officials in the AME Church, that is, bishops, district superintendents, and presiding elders, were male, Riley needed their protection and an open-door policy to succeed. Earlier black women preachers had neither.

In 1809, about four or five years after her conversion to Christianity and while a member of Bethel Church in Philadelphia,[45] Jarena Lee writes that she approached her pastor, the Reverend Richard Allen, and informed him that she believed she was called to preach:

> I now told him, that the Lord had revealed it to me, that I must preach the gospel. He replied by asking, in what *sphere* I wished to move in? I said, among the Methodists. He then replied, that a Mrs. Cook, a Methodist lady, had also some time before requested the same privilege; who it was believed, had done much good in the way of exhortation, and holding prayer meetings; and who had been permitted to do so by *verbal license* of the preacher in charge at the time. But as to women preaching, he said that *our Discipline* knew nothing at all about it—*that it did not call for women preachers.*[46]

Throughout her life, Lee worked tirelessly to gain formal recognition from male church leadership, created alternative spaces in people's homes and communities to share the gospel she fervently believed she was called to preach, and helped to change the perceptions male preachers had about their future female colleagues.

It is clear from various minutes of the South Carolina Conference of the AME Church that women were not being employed as leaders of the denomination as late as the 1870s, more than fifty years after the Church's founding. Typically, women's names are excluded from the conference proceedings except where they are listed as financial contributors to a particular department. Charlotte Riley and her coworker Emily Rodney (who later adopted the surname Williams after marriage) are the only women listed in the conference records as leading missionaries. During the Missionary Society meeting of February 1, 1871, Riley and Rodney were elected as life members of the society in "consideration of their earnest, faithful and efficent [*sic*] labors as missionaries."[47] In subsequent annual conference minutes, they are permanently listed as officers of the conference, the only women listed as such.

Toward the end of her narrative, Riley ponders her pioneering role:

> Well, I have been an acceptable member in their midst since 1871, laboring for the supply of the church and gaining of souls, with all credit to my calling, irrespective of standing or creed, and the secret in my holding up and out these many years is trusting in God to carry on His plans and leave the ranting to the formalist . . . and to do this I have labored earnestly and believingly, and as strong as is my faith in the Word of God, keeping in mind it is better to live long in the Gospel to the honor of God, as no one will thank you for killing yourself by ranting out the message of the Lord, and when you are dead, men will call you a fool. I have heard their murmurings, after receiving the message of such, saying they were unbenefitted, occupying the time over the loquacity of the messenger. I don't believe it is the way God's message is to be delivered. I believe that what I am is of more importance than what I do, and the providence of God makes me responsible for the careful preservation and proper use of the powers granted. I have no right to needlessly throw away the energy which God has granted me. As God's messengers, you and I, dear reader of this class, have a right, I believe it a duty as well, to guard against excess and avoid danger and to abstain from everything which can injure or destroy us. There is no one to care for me as I can for myself, so I have tried and always will to have food, raiment, rest, sleep and protection so to befit myself for the best and most lasting service for the glory of God and the good of mankind. Praise the Lord, Amen.[48]

Riley began writing her autobiography in 1896, when she was fifty-seven years old. Unbroken in zeal with "lungs as sound as a girl's," the preacher has become wise with experience after years of service. She speaks directly to those who might follow her—other preaching women, perhaps—and argues for self-preservation. She advises those who undertake the herculean task of laboring in spiritual and secular public service to work smart, get plenty of rest, eat well, and trust God to fulfill the work He has ordained. Ultimately, she concludes that the emphasis should not be on loquacity or long sermons. That should be left to the ranting formalist. Instead, she squarely places her faith in God's word to ensure victory. Her narrative ends with up-to-the-minute accounts of her work: letters from colleagues and protégés, a response from the third assistant postmaster general concerning her inquiry about Roosevelt's visit to Lincolnville, and information from local news sources referencing her work—all testaments to her success and continued vigor. However, her message to those coming behind her is clear: taking care of one's self is paramount in ministry and is accomplished only by the minister herself.

Alongside the challenges of gender inequity, the threat of racial violence intruded on Riley's preaching work in the Reconstruction years of the 1870s. She relates an incident that occurred in Spartanburg, South Carolina, which is about two hundred miles from Charleston. She received word upon her arrival to preach in the city that a white citizen of the town had invited the host pastor to hold the services at the courthouse so that the white townspeople could attend, since the host church would be too small to accommodate the larger crowd. The pastor accepted the invitation. When the courthouse bell rang to notify the citizens of the hour of service, it also notified the "common whites," who were "dressed in blood red shirts, carrying Winchesters, [and] preparing for the great Democratic campaign meeting on the next day."[49] While the date of the event is unclear, the existence of the Red Shirts as a paramilitary group designed to instill fear in those who did not support the Democratic Party is well documented, particularly the group's determination to regain control of local and state offices from black and white Republicans in 1876 in parts of North and South Carolina. Despite the presence of federal troops in some areas, various groups of mounted Democrats wearing red shirts rode through the streets of South Carolina communities to intimidate black voters before the November election of that year. On voting day, November 7, hundreds of black voters were turned away from the polls. Fearlessly, Riley preached to a packed house from Galatians 6:17, "Let no man trouble me, for I bear in my body the marks of the Lord Jesus." Sympathetic whites, probably Republicans whom Riley refers to as "citizens," had anticipated potential resistance and intimidation, prompting them to move the services to the state building and preempt any potential violence. Their progressive thinking protected Riley and the church members. As she prepared to leave the next day at the train depot, some of the sympathetic white community members assured her that they would be pleased to have her return. Riley's appropriation of Paul's words to the Galatians provided her with the necessary weapon she needed to stave off danger. Like both the innocent, suffering Christ and the powerful Apostle Paul, Riley was prepared to meet the challenges of ministry and racial discrimination.

The community organizer was also approached by nonreligious black leaders to help with the concerns of newly emancipated black people. In 1868, she organized a group of local sharecroppers to help them make a profit on their cotton crops; in 1869, she assisted Isaac Myers, the president of the Colored National Labor Union, to elect delegates for the Colored National Labor Convention to be held in Washington, DC, in December of that year. In 1876, Riley received a request from the Honorable Robert Brown Elliott (1842–84), a lawyer, journalist, US congressman, and the first African American commanding general of the South Carolina National Guard, to "make a call for the men and organize a militia" in advance of the upcoming Democratic and Republican South Carolina conventions. Elliot anticipated violence because of the controversial nature of the election. Riley helped to organize the militia and made banners: "We fought for our liberty" and "The Negro has come to stay with you white men." She, along with her missionary coworker, Emily Rodney, was invited to attend the convention by the AME bishop Richard Cain, the noted religious and political leader. Riley mused that the convention delegates

> used their liberty to choose for themselves which is the right party for them to follow, and which the wrong, as it was their liberty to execute it, but as the years go by what changes have we not seen, of trials and conflict, with the experience of victory and defeat in the warfare of right against wrong, the strong against the weak, the rich against the poor, intelligence against ignorance. With the knowledge of these noted facts before my mind's eye, constrained me to hard labor the best I could to obtain the knowledge of books, coupled with the "Gift of God," which no man living or dead could take away.[50]

Quite impressively for a Reconstruction-era black woman, Riley became financially stable and owned two houses and a four-acre lot. In 1883, Riley's doctor advised her to move where she could rest, warning her that otherwise she would not recover her "usual little strength." She decided to sell her land in Columbia and relocate to the newly formed town of Lincolnville, which had been established by Bishop Richard Cain and six other men in 1867. The town was incorporated in 1889. The proliferation of all-black incorporated towns after the Civil War signaled African Americans' desire to create safe spaces within which they could secure homes, churches, community organizations, and, perhaps most irksome for whites resentful of black independence, businesses

Ebenezer AME Church, Lincolnville, SC, ca. 1900 (photo courtesy of Rev. Anna Ruth Williams-Gleaton)

for their newly freed families.[51] During her stay in Lincolnville, Riley faced many challenges to her health. She broke her arm, was on crutches for a period, and continued to suffer with migraines. Yet she continued her extensive travel throughout the state of South Carolina and became a mentor to future black leaders. For Riley, Lincolnville served as her "headquarters," the place to which she continually returned to rest after her preaching campaigns and political activism. She served faithfully as a member of the Ebenezer AME Church, the first house of worship erected in the village by Bishop Cain and the town's early founders. As her work continued, in 1885 Riley was appointed as the town's postmistress. The following year she helped to aid Charleston's victims of the worst earthquake in the history of the southeastern United States. She went on crutches to "dispense to them God's sure words of promise." In 1902, Riley's letter-writing campaign helped to influence President Theodore Roosevelt to visit the Lincolnville/Summerville area during his trip to the Charleston Exposition, better known as the World's Fair. It is clear that the work of supporting, educating, and ministering to black people in Reconstruction South

Ebenezer AME Church, Lincolnville, SC, 2015 (photo courtesy of T. L. Lucky)

Carolina happened within a fluid environment, where political and labor leaders, ministers, and educators, who were often one and the same, worked together with limited resources but great strength of resolve and purpose: to achieve racial and social equality.

There are many reasons why *The Autobiography: A Mysterious Life and Calling* should be read at this contemporary moment. The expanding circle of black preaching and writing women whose work scholars are restoring to the canon of American arts and letters is inspiring. The body of work produced by nineteenth-century African American women writers and speakers points to their existence as a strong, productive, and diverse group essential to the spiritual, political, and social progress of black people from the period of American chattel slavery to their admittance in the acknowledged citizenry of the nation and clerical ranks of the church. Charlotte Riley offers compelling evidence of her fruitful preaching career, life of public service, and commitment to social and moral uplift. She possessed amazing physical stamina and sacrificed her personal comfort, even risking her health, to help her wider community, and she was willing to travel miles and miles to preach to large and small congregations of blacks and whites, women and men, and former slaves and former slaveholders in established churches and private homes. She did so in the face of challenges thrown to black women aspiring to gain access to formal clerical leadership. Her ability to traverse the state of South Carolina freely to do the work of the AME Church is, in large part, due to the establishment of her preaching and teaching ministry after the close of the Civil War.

Perhaps most important is the recovery of an additional text to the growing corpus of material about American slavery. Riley's relative privilege afforded her an education that prepared her to think and write about her life's experiences in ways that others afflicted by slavery's shackles were simply unable to do. Although her daily life in slavery was not characterized by physical abuse, sexual violation, or material deprivation, she was a slave who witnessed emancipation and lived to write about it. Readers are cautioned not to interpret American slavery, its aftermath or millions of victims, through a lens of homogeneity. Each narrator reveals his or her particular experience but nevertheless adds to a nuanced, layered, and complex collective story of the black experience on American soil. Riley's ability to overcome the stigma of slavery, the deaths of her family members, poor health, and abandonment by her husband speaks to her great personal fortitude.

Finally and perhaps most pragmatically, the text offers an invaluable repository of information for students of South Carolina, Reconstruction, and AME Church history. Riley lists over 150 names of individuals she lived and worshipped with, worked for, or admired as public figures. This new edition of Riley's narrative has been carefully and painstakingly annotated and indexed. For those interested in tracing family or institutional histories, the text potentially provides important missing links. Her narrative remains relevant and contributes to our growing understanding of black spiritual and secular life writing.

———

The text's original spelling, punctuation, paragraphing, and section divisions have been preserved, except for letters and newspaper articles, which have been extracted for readability. All footnotes in the text are provided by the editor. All biblical passages have been quoted from the King James Version of the Bible.

NOTES

1. In the Betrayal of 1877, better known as the Compromise of 1877, which assured the election of the Republican candidate, Rutherford B. Hayes, as president, Democrats brokered a deal that left formerly enslaved black Southerners abandoned and signaled the end of Reconstruction. For a discussion of the devastating effects of the agreement, see Eric Foner, *Reconstruction: America's Unfinished Revolution, 1863–1877* (New York: Harper & Row, 1988); Jackson Lears, *Rebirth of a Nation: The Making of Modern America, 1877–1920* (New York: HarperCollins, 2009); and Brenda Wineapple, *Ecstatic Nation: Confidence, Crisis, and Compromise, 1848–1877* (New York: HarperCollins, 2013).

2. Bishop Levi Jenkins Coppin (1848–1923) was elected as the thirtieth bishop of the AME Church. He served as the editor of the *A.M.E. Review* from 1888 to 1896; pastor of the historic Mother Bethel AME Church in Philadelphia, Pennsylvania, from 1896 to 1900; and bishop of the Fourteenth Episcopal District in South Africa and later the Seventh Episcopal District, which encompassed South Carolina and Alabama. He was also the husband of the noted educator and lecturer Fannie Jackson Coppin (1837–1913).

3. Daniel Joseph Jenkins (1853–1937) was a pastor and business owner who founded the Orphan Aid Society and later the Orphan Industrial Farm, which became known as the Jenkins Orphanage Institute. During his lifetime, the institute provided shelter and training to over five thousand boys and girls. Jenkins organized some of the children into a band that helped raise money for and brought notoriety to the organization. The band played at the inaugural parades of both Presidents Theodore Roosevelt (1905) and William Taft (1909). To support the institute, Jenkins also purchased a printing press and published works by local authors, including Charlotte Riley, and a weekly newspaper, the *Charleston Messenger*. For more on Jenkins, see Walter J. Frazer, *Charleston! Charleston! The History of a Southern City* (Columbia: University of South Carolina Press, 1989); and Martin Abbott, "The Freedman's Bureau and Negro Schooling in South Carolina," *South Carolina Historical Magazine* 57 (April 1956): 65–81. See also http://www.jenkinsinstitute.org.

4. There were at least two black preaching women of the nineteenth century who were born into slavery and published their life's stories: Sojourner Truth, née Isabella Bomfree; and Amanda Berry Smith. However, Riley's Southern narrative is unique because *The Narrative of Sojourner Truth*, dictated to Olive Gilbert in 1850, describes Truth's experiences with New York slavery. Additionally, Amanda Berry Smith was born into slavery in Maryland in 1837, but her father purchased the family's freedom when Smith was only three years old. Thus, neither Smith's development nor her narrative was characterized by the slave community or a master-slave relationship. See Margaret Washington, ed., *Narrative of Sojourner Truth* (New York: Vintage Books, 1993); and Amanda Berry Smith, *An Autobiography: The Story of the Lord's Dealings with Mrs. Amanda Smith the Colored Evangelist*, ed. Henry Louis Gates Jr., with an introduction by Jualynne E. Dodson (New York: Oxford University Press, 1988).

5. See Ira Berlin, *Generations of Captivity: A History of African American Slaves* (Cambridge, MA: Harvard University Press, 2003); and Barbara Jeanne Fields, *Slavery and Freedom on Middle Ground: Maryland during the Nineteenth Century* (New Haven, CT: Yale University Press, 1985).

6. For a more complete discussion of Charleston's antebellum black community, see Bernard E. Powers Jr., *Black Charlestonians: A Social History, 1822–1885* (Fayetteville: University of Arkansas Press, 1994), 9–35.

7. Ibid., 136. For a discussion of South Carolina law forbidding black literacy, see William Goodell, *The American Slave Code in Theory and Practice: Its Distinctive Features Shown by Its Statues, Judicial Decisions, and Illustrative Facts*, 3rd ed. (New York: American and Foreign Anti-Slavery Society, 1853), 319–25. For a discussion of antebellum and Reconstruction black education in the South, with emphasis on South Carolina, see Heather Andrea Williams, *Self-Taught: African American Education in Slavery and Freedom* (Chapel Hill: University of North Carolina Press, 2005), 80–95, 96–125; Powers, *Black Charlestonians*, 136–59; Abbott, "The Freedman's Bureau," 65–81; C. W. Birnie, "Education of the Negro in Charleston, South Carolina Prior to the Civil War," *Journal of Negro History* 12 (January 1927): 13–21; Laylon W. Jordan, "Education for Community: C. G. Memminger and the Origination of Common Schools in Antebellum Charleston," *South Carolina Historical Magazine* 83 (April 1982): 99–115; and James D. Anderson, *The Education of Blacks in the South, 1860–1935* (Chapel Hill: University of North Carolina Press, 1988).

8. See pages 35–36.

9. See page 54.

10. Harriet Jacobs, *Incidents in the Life of a Slave Girl Written by Herself*, ed. and with an introduction by Jean Fagan Yellin (Cambridge, MA: Harvard University Press, 1988), 5.

11. See page 40.

12. See Susie King Taylor, *Reminiscences of My Life in Camp with the 33d United States Colored Troops Late 1st South Carolina Volunteers* (Boston: The author, 1902).

13. Powers, *Black Charlestonians*, 41–46.

14. See page 40.

15. See page 42.

16. See Robert M. Weir, *Colonial South Carolina: A History* (Millwood, NY: KTO Press, 1983), 173, 177, 328–30. See also Edward Ball, *Slaves in the Family* (New York: Ballantine, 1999); and Cindy Lee, *A Tour of Historic Sullivan's Island* (Charleston, SC: History Press, 2010).

17. Nineteenth-century black women's spiritual autobiographies have gained a great deal of deserved attention in the past twenty-five years. The recovery of significant primary sources along with the repositioning of black women's writing to the fore of literary critical scholarship has led scholars to reconsider the importance of the African American autobiographical narrative, generally, and the black preaching woman's narrative, specifically, to early black literature. Nineteenth-century black women's writing continues to yield important revelations about women's experience and their varied struggles to increase their influence despite the restrictions placed on them due to color, class, and sex. Significant primary sources collected early in the recovery process include William Andrews's collection of the narratives of Jarena Lee, Zilpha Elaw and Julia Foote, *Sisters of the Spirit: Three Black Women's Autobiographies of the Nineteenth Century* (Bloomington: Indiana University Press, 1986); Marilyn Richardson's collection of the public speeches and spiritual musings of Maria Stewart, *Maria W. Stewart, America's First Black Woman Political Writer* (Bloomington: Indiana University Press,

1987); the expanded journal of Jarena Lee, reprinted in Maria W. Stewart et al., *Spiritual Narratives*, Schomburg Library of Nineteenth-Century Black Women Writers (New York: Oxford University Press, 1988); and Margaret Washington's critical edition of Sojourner Truth's dictated narrative, *Narrative of Sojourner Truth* (New York: Vintage Books, 1993). A wealth of scholarship and additional recovery has ensued: Nellie McKay, "Nineteenth-Century Black Women's Spiritual Autobiographies: Religious Faith and Self-Empowerment," in *Interpreting Women's Lives: Feminist Theory and Personal Narratives*, ed. Personal Narratives Group (Bloomington: Indiana University Press, 1989); Joanne Braxton, *Black Women Writing Autobiography: A Tradition within A Tradition* (Philadelphia: Temple University Press, 1990); Frances Smith Foster, *Written by Herself: Literary Production by African American Women, 1746–1892* (Bloomington: Indiana University Press, 1993); Evelyn Brooks Higginbotham, *Righteous Discontent: The Women's Movement in the Black Baptist Church, 1880–1920* (Cambridge, MA: Harvard University Press, 1993); Carla Peterson, *"Doers of the Word": African American Women Speakers and Writers in the North (1830–1880)* (New York: Oxford University Press, 1995); Nell Irvin Painter, *Sojourner Truth: A Life, a Symbol* (New York: W. W. Norton, 1996); Bettye Collier-Thomas, *Daughters of Thunder: Black Women Preachers and Their Sermons, 1850–1979* (San Francisco: Jossey-Bass, 1998); Katherine Bassard, *Spiritual Interrogations: Culture, Gender, and Community in Early African American Women's Writing* (Princeton, NJ: Princeton University Press, 1999); Richard J. Douglass-Chin, *Preacher Woman Sings the Blues: The Autobiographies of Nineteenth-Century African American Evangelists* (Columbia: University of Missouri Press, 2001); Joycelyn Moody, *Sentimental Confessions: Spiritual Narratives of Nineteenth-Century African American Women* (Athens: University of Georgia Press, 2001); Chanta M. Haywood, *Prophesying Daughters: Black Women Preachers and the Word, 1823–1913* (Columbia: University of Missouri Press, 2003); John Ernest, *Liberation Historiography: African American Writers and the Challenge of History, 1794–1861* (Chapel Hill: University of North Carolina Press, 2004) and *Chaotic Justice: Rethinking African American Literary History* (Chapel Hill: University of North Carolina Press, 2009); Cedrick May, *Evangelism and Resistance in the Black Atlantic, 1760–1835* (Athens: University of Georgia Press, 2008); Susanna Ashton, ed., *I Belong to South Carolina: South Carolina Slave Narratives* (Columbia: University of South Carolina Press, 2010); and Rhondda Robinson Thomas and Susanna Ashton, eds., *The South Carolina Roots of African American Thought: A Reader* (Columbia: University of South Carolina Press, 2014).

18. A. Smith, *An Autobiography*, iii, emphasis mine.

19. Andrews, *Sisters of the Spirit*, 55.

20. Ibid., 51–160.

21. Jean Humez, ed., *The Writings of Rebecca Jackson: Black Visionary, Shaker Eldress* (Amherst: University of Massachusetts Press, 1987), 71.

22. Ibid.

23. Her conversion led her on a lifelong quest for holiness that took her first to the AME Church and then to the predominantly white Shakers. Because sexual intimacy did not fit with her understanding of living a "Christ-like life," eventually Jackson left her husband and retreated outside of the boundaries of traditional religious circles to form her own eclectic group, composed of women.

24. Stewart et al., *Spiritual Narratives*, xxxvii–xxxviii.

25. Peterson, *"Doers of the Word,"* 80.

26. This difficulty would have been true for fugitive slave narrators as well. Valerie Smith argues that Harriet Jacobs's detailed description of her small garret space served as a metaphor for the "structures of concealment" and "evasion" in nineteenth-century black women's writing that reflected "the limited cultural options available to the authors because of their gender" and sociopolitical positions. See Valerie Smith, "'Loopholes of Retreat': Architecture and Ideology in Harriet Jacobs' *Incidents in the Life of a Slave Girl*," in *Reading Black, Reading Feminist: A Critical Anthology*, ed. Henry Louis Gates Jr. (New York: Meridian Books, 1990), 214.

27. Bassard, *Spiritual Interrogations*, 124.

28. See page 66.

29. Andrews, *Sisters of the Spirit*, 88–89.

30. See page 59.

31. Andrews, *Sisters of the Spirit*, 27, 89.

32. Ibid., 196.

33. A. Smith, *An Autobiography*, 57.

34. Darlene Clark Hine, ed., *Black Women in America*, 2nd ed. (New York: Oxford University Press, 2005), 453–54.

35. A. Smith, *An Autobiography*, 58.

36. Ann duCille, *The Coupling Convention: Sex, Text, and Tradition in Black Women's Fiction* (New York: Oxford University Press, 1993), 4–5, 31.

37. Ibid., 31.

38. A. Smith, *An Autobiography*, 96.

39. See page 50.

40. See page 51.

41. Methodist class leaders are appointed annually by the pastor of the local church to oversee a class of at least twelve members. The class is formed to meet weekly, provide instruction in the doctrine and discipline of the AME Church, support the members, and receive their monetary contributions. Class leaders report to the official board and recommend the class members for full church membership after ninety days. See *The Doctrine and Discipline of the African Methodist Episcopal Church* (Philadelphia: AME Book Concern, 1885).

42. See page 64.

43. See page 68.

44. See page 93.

45. Now called Mother Bethel, the historic church remains at its original location at 6th and Lombard Streets in South Philadelphia. Members from the African Free Society established both St. Thomas Episcopal Church, then pastored by Absalom Jones and now located near Lancaster and City Line Avenues in Philadelphia, and Bethel Church within months of each other in 1794.

46. Andrews, *Sisters of the Spirit*, 36, emphasis mine.

47. Minutes of the Second Session of the Columbia, South Carolina, Conference of the African Methodist Episcopal Church, February 1, 1871, published 1872.

48. See pages 93–94.
49. See page 70.
50. See page 77.
51. For a complete discussion on the proliferation of all-black incorporated towns during the nineteenth century, see Christine W. Hampton and Rosalee W. Washington, *The History of Lincolnville, South Carolina* (Charleston: BookSurge, 2007); Tim Madigan, *The Burning: Massacre, Destruction, and Tulsa Race Riot of 1921* (New York: St. Martin's, 2001); Nell Irvin Painter, *Exodusters: Black Migration to Kansas after Reconstruction* (New York: W. W. Norton, 1986); and Thomas Holt, *Black over White: Negro Political Leadership in South Carolina during Reconstruction* (Urbana: University of Illinois Press, 1979).

The Autobiography

A MYSTERIOUS LIFE AND CALLING

$\mathcal{B}$e it known to all who may chance to read this little work, put up in the form of a book. It is not the choice of the writer, but simply to comply with the request of my many admiring friends of all classes, believing as they have so urgently told me that the work will be an incentive to some young, ambitious, yet fearful heart. With such expressions of confidence and interest, I decided to make an effort to write the work. Trusting their opinion in the matter, that it may do good to some one, "as good doth the upright in heart."[1] However, I may run into the hand of the critical world; but the admirers and sympathisers say: write, for surely we can produce from our side of the stage an actor in merit and in labors of love — a true exemplar, a mysterious character, worthy to be noted by the actor upon the stage of life." Believing the apology made is seen and understood by all intelligent readers of this little book, I feel myself at liberty to write, leaving my case into the hands of those who constrained me to make this attempt at writing up my life so full of mystery, (Amen).

Reverently yours,

C. S. RILEY.

---

1. The quotation paraphrases Psalm 125:4: "Do good, O LORD, unto those that be good, and to them that are upright in their hearts." All biblical quotations are taken from the King James Version of the Bible.

With the Author

Voltaire I see, "That the more we have read and have meditated, the better conditioned we are to affirm that we know nothing."[2] These expressions extract much of my willingness for doing that I would not. Well, after giving the matter my serious consideration, I have consented to give the events of my life, as I can recall the many victories won over evil pursuers, destroyers of goodness and virtue, such as have been destructive to many who would have achieved a grand and useful life. You know as well as I do, that there is no attraction in the character of the man slayer, "he may battle his way and ascend the ladder of fame, but the mark of blood on him remain." My boast, however, of victory over these oppositions may inspire some anxious seeker after friendship with his Maker, it may strengthen the feeble mind and give hope to the poor and cast down to arise and ascend the hill of difficulty and reflect the honor of his maker, God—glory to the Most Highest.

The writer was born in Charleston, S. C., on the 26th August, 1839, of poor slave parents. This prevented them to render unto their only girl child born to them the assistance necessary in preparing her for the end to which she was born. It seemed, however, to have been the hope of their mind that God's way was too great a mystery "for them to lose their trust in—but they would wait God's will to perform and his purposes to ripen,"[3] while their child was maturing up to womanhood, as they held in their mind that their only girl's peculiar birth potend [sic] to some special event in life's work. They said as a child I displayed a superior spirit beyond my four brothers. My love for books and letters were far beyond my age. My parents although poor and slaves, had great advantage, far beyond their fellows, as being allowed to hire their time at five to

2. Voltaire, quoted (with some minor changes here) in *A Dictionary of Thoughts: Being a Cyclopedia of Laconic Quotations from the Best Authors of the World, Both Ancient and Modern* (New York: Cassell, 1891), ed. Tryon Edwards, D. D. (1809–94). Edwards was the great-great-grandson of the Reverend Jonathan Edwards, the noted revivalist preacher of the First Great Awakening.

3. The quotation is likely from stanzas 1 and 5 of the British hymn writer William Cowper's (1731–1800) "God Moves in a Mysterious Way" (1773): "God moves in a mysterious way, His wonders to perform / He plants His footsteps in the sea, And rides upon the storm / His purposes will ripen fast, Unfolding every hour / The bud may have a bitter taste, But sweet will be the flower."

ten dollars per month, according to their value, with free rented homes to themselves, with their children under their care until they were grown to years of usefulness. So the opportunity came, that a little aid could be given the children, and their little girl was considered. However, the law of the State was very rigid against the slaves being taught to read and write. The children, however, were allowed to attend such schools as would teach the girls and boys some trade that would be of profit to their owners. So I was sent to a sewing school kept to teach the art of the needle as a support for the family, she being a respectable woman of freedom, the widow Duncan. The Elder —— kept her class of pupils on the first floor, where the needle went trimbly all day from 9 a. m., with a little recess at twelve and to dinner at two, and return at three until six p. m. The young ladies kept their school upstairs, and at a certain hour the down stairs pupils would be sent up to the young ladies' room to recite their lessons. Our books were kept up there, so you see we had to keep two sets of the old Thomas Dillworth [*sic*] Primer, with the New York Reader, and the Testament.[4] We were sent in turn to figure the examples set by the teacher on the board. You will see as you read and think of the stride of the negro of to-day and the alarm caused by their rapid march toward the hilltop of learning. Why, the law, in the beginning, forbade its aid in grasping the hand of the negro, the unconquerable weapon, the sword of knowledge. You will also see the cause of the prevalent accusation of the negro deception and deceit. Can you not see in a nutshell the principle of the school of his graduation, this school of oppression, has taught the oppressed to contrive a way for relief, and this is all in the case of the oppressed and the oppressor. This little girl, however, lost no time to learn that her soul longed for light. My parents said I made rapid progress in my books, as far as my health allowed me, as I was born a slave to disease, having

4. The students' use of the old Dilworth primer indicates the economic challenges under which small privately run schools for slave children operated. From the mid-eighteenth century until the Revolution, the most popular schoolbooks in the colonies were the primer, grammar, and arithmetic of the Englishman Thomas Dilworth. However, after the Revolutionary War, Dilworth's student Noah Webster printed his own primer, which became the standard schoolbook for nineteenth-century Americans. Interestingly, Abraham Lincoln learned to read using Dilworth's primer, which imparted moral lessons alongside the grammatical. See Marie Updegraff, "Education Spelled Freedom," in *Stamford, Past and Present* (Stamford: Stamford Bicentennial Committee, 1976), available on the website of the Stamford Historical Society, http://www.cslib.org/stamford/pp_ed.htm.

inherited nervous headache: you would not be so far away from the point to call it disease of the brain.[5] This gave the title rightly, as we have it, "A Mysterious Life and Calling." Poor health forbade my regular attendance at school, however anxious I was to be there. Strange as it may seem for the afflicted head, I could always retain in mind that which I had received. My memory was, and is still, astonishingly strong. I was born with the spirit of utilitarian, and could never believe that the system of it is not "the good, the profitable, useful life." Strange life, indeed; I could never hurry or move in any excitement: those under whose care I was in had from necessity to deal with me very gently and all who came in contact with me seemed to understand the nature of my case all through childhood, up to the present age of womanhood. At the age of fourteen I was mysteriously converted to the religion of the Lord Jesus, on Sullivan's Island,[6] at an old time Methodist watch-night meeting. You question what is the mystery in the conversion? Be patient, and I shall tell you. I had a vision like this: I was spending a while with a friend, Miss Myra Rivers,[7] a young Christian, who was quite interested in my soul. I could not see the need of a change. I held myself good enough. But I was resting upon morality, because I had not reasoned otherwise. I could not see the use of her shouting at meeting,

5. In the mid-nineteenth century, the condition was also referred to as neurasthenia, neurotic, stress, or hysterical headache, a psychopathological term first used in 1869 by the Yale College–trained physician George Miller Beard (1839–83) to denote a condition with symptoms of fatigue, anxiety, headache, neuralgia, and depression. Dr. Beard attributed the illness to patients' failure to adapt to the increasing demands of urbanization and their attempt to achieve more than their constitution could cope with. The label of neurasthenia was applied to a whole range of physical and mental symptoms, including anxiety, despair, phobias, insomnia, inattention, extreme fatigue, palpitations, migraines, indigestion, and impotence. Many of women's unexplained symptoms were categorized as such. Riley's narrative indicates that she suffered with the condition throughout her life. See Marijke Gijswijt-Hofstra, "Neurasthenia," in *Encyclopedia of Disability*, vol. 3, ed. Gary L. Albrecht (Thousand Oaks, CA: Sage Reference, 2006), 1139–40; and Diane Price Herndl, "The Invisible (Invalid) Woman: African-American Women, Illness and Nineteenth-Century Narrative," *Women's Studies* 24 (1995): 553–72.

6. For a full discussion of the significance of Sullivan's Island, see the introduction. See also Ball, *Slaves in the Family*; and Lee, *A Tour of Historic Sullivan's Island*.

7. One of the major contributions of Riley's narrative is that she names more than 155 different black and white individuals associated with Charleston society, public service, and the Methodist, Methodist Episcopal, African Methodist Episcopal, Presbyterian, and Baptist church denominations. Some are identified in South Carolina census and death records.

and was quite a pest to her on the matter. However, she prayed God should make me see the need. Do you wonder at this, dear reader? When you know I had nothing to shout for. Well, one beautiful moonlight night, indeed, this is reality, we enjoyed the delightful evening out on the stoop until drowsiness overtook us, and we retired to bed, and in the vision of my mind; a man came in the door and up to my bedside and spoke to me with an authority to be obeyed, "Get up and come with me." I arose and put on my slippers and went to the door to see what—the moon was still up shining as I left it to go to bed. "Follow me," he said. And I followed—couldn't help it, drawn as I were as by magnetism. So he led me through a beautiful passage up to a beautiful building, into a spacious room, and as I entered I heard the most melodious, inspiring songs. The man said to me, "Join in the song, and shout around." "Oh, no," said I, "for I don't believe in the exercise." So he sang and joined in with the assembly, and before I knew who I was I was among the shouters and had to be taken away, as the last one of the assembly. The very man was with me on all occasions. They took me safely through the moonlight back to my rooms, and as we got up to the door he spoke to me like this, "Now, I want you to meet me at the same house about three weeks from to-night." I could do no more nor less than to consent to meet him again in that very pleasant and enjoyable association of persons. Then he wanted a pledge. As a trial of my sincerity, he says, "Suppose it rains frogs?" "Sir, I shall come." "Well, suppose the two tides shall meet?" "Sir, I shall come." As it was not an uncommon thing at a spring tide for the tide of the front beach to overflow its borders and meet the tide of the back beach, dividing the upper part of the land from the lower; passage could only be made by vehicles. Three weeks have passed, and the fatal day is here: the third week Saturday of September, one among its sweetest days, and a day of my life never to me forgotten. There was a knock at the gate. My friend goes to see who they were. She came in with an old church leader of the people, by name Brother George Doewell, "informing the members as the proprietor of the meeting" that they are "assessed 25 cents to meet the expenses of the watch night to be held in the upper part of the village" on that night. Surely my 25 cents was in with his members, as the revelation of the vision was drawing near, and as all of the house had been told the singular vision, had with me grown anxious.

It was ten a. m. when the old man came, and I was kept in a state of anxiety all the day long, however it was a lovely day with no sign of suspicion. At twelve o'clock, the sun shone out in its meridian beauty. The heavenly watch seemed to say as a solace, "all is well," and I began to feel hopeful again.

The suspense of the mind brought me to a point of reasoning. O! how my mind ascended to a height in imagining. What shall be the case, shall I be disappointed, and must meet my obligation as pledged to the peculiarly strange man, until I ascended the sky, and thought of the "home of God, my Maker," and wondered will I ever get there and how shall I get there? My poor health kept me from all compulsory labors, so I were reclining all the day, and the hour passed unnoticed.

Until the clock surprised me that it was after four. Miss Rivers, my friend, came in just at this time. How things looked out there, I asked? All is right, says she, and some of our best local men will be upon the seven o'clock boat from the city, "and a grand time is looked for."

Do you know their names? I asked her.

Oh, yes. "Mr. Joshua Wilson, the man after God's own heart," and the Saviour's own man, Mr. James Dart. Mr. Nelson Richardson, "the Lion of the Tribe," and your own dear "papa," the Paul of the number, who will do or die for the cause of his Master.

"So we are to have a shouting in the camp tonight?" O, how I wished with her I could understand the shouting in the camp.

While we were hoping for the night, "Sister Talton called to the door, look out here, and we hastened to see, what? Why there is a patch of black cloud in the west the size of a pillow, and out of that small patch the lightnings were playing like the boys' rockets, and in about an hour from that the whole heavens were as black as midnight, and the thundering was fearful.

The passengers on the last boat, with God's workmen, just made their escape out of a pouring rain that truly brought down the frogs, with the two tides meeting. So true, poor me, the whole house were doing their best to soothe my cares, but determined will to fulfill my words, so sure was I all would be well with me, live or die, in my attempt. What do you say—"Ignorant?" Can I declare to you in such a glaring demonstration and revelation of the vision of my soul?

No, God bless you, no fearing, no doubting, "with Christ on my side," I shall go to meet my promise "trusting my Lord to provide."

The dear friends tried to make me see that my willingness to obey will be accepted as doing, but my mind was to form to see point, but like the faithful Paul, I "had pledged to go—though death awaited my going."[8] O, mysterious

8. A reference to Acts 20:22–24, which describes the Apostle Paul's determination to go to Jerusalem during his third missionary tour not knowing what would befall him during his journey or once he arrived.

life, led by a mysterious God, with the storm unabated, and hope had almost gone.

With no one outside knowing our troubles, or to give to us aid. Here a coach comes up to the door of the big house in search of a passenger, "who wanted to leave the island on the first boat for the city." As my friend had to attend the call, and gave the answer to the coachman, she took the chance to engage him to return, and take us to the meeting. So he returned at eleven o'clock and took us through the rain and the tides safely to the place. O, matchless working God, mysterious indeed, as soon as we were safely housed, the rain abated, and the full moon shone out in her queenly beauty, as though the clouds had never "shut her in its pillow of blackness."

Surely the meeting was a grand success. According to promise the Holy Spirit met me on my return from the mercy seat.[9] The Spirit touched me, and I fell in the passage way to my seat in a swoon of transportation, and was carried to the home of my friend, and for three days I was abiding in a world of love and glory., having died to sin and made alive unto the knowledge of "Christ and Him crucified."[10]

"Washed in the blood of the Lamb, Hallelujah! I am saved from the transgression of the law." Can't I shout as I come out of the wilderness "holding on to my Lord?"[11] Shouting "Glory, I am saved, and saved forever, in Jesus' Name."

9. The Mercy Seat comprised the covering of the Ark of the Covenant, which held the Ten Commandments God gave to Moses in the wilderness. Made of solid gold, the seat was flanked on either side by two gold cherubim that faced each other and whose wings covered the seat. The Ark of the Covenant and the Mercy Seat were located in the innermost sanctuary of the tabernacle in the wilderness, called "the Holy of Holies" or "the Holiest of All," and was only allowed to be accessed by the High Priest. Metaphorically, Riley envisions her salvation experience in terms of the Mercy Seat and God's promise to visit and commune with Israel: "And there I will meet with thee, and I will commune with thee from above the mercy seat, from between the two cherubim which are upon the ark of the testimony, of all things which I will give thee in commandment unto the children of Israel" (Exodus 25:22). See Exodus 25:17–21 and Hebrews 9:1–5.

10. Riley freely adopts biblical language and the writing style of the Apostle Paul, integrating and liberally quoting familiar phrases from his epistles. In this instance, she is likely referring to a combination of Romans 6:6–11 and 1 Corinthians 2:1–2.

11. A reference to the folk song/Negro spiritual "How Did You Feel?": "How did you feel when you come out the wilderness, come out the wilderness, come out the wilderness? How did you feel when you come out the wilderness, leaning on the Lord?"

On my return to the city I took up my membership in the Presbyterian Church, under the leadership of Mr. Richard Townsend, uncle to the noted Rev. Alonzo Townsend, of the M. E. Church. I was blest with the implicit confidence of my friends toward me, as in these repeated calls on me to positions of trust. From young womanhood I was chosen as a teacher of the Sabbath School Class among the Northern teachers of the Avery Institute.[12] Many boys and girls have been disciplined under my charge. Some have gone to join in with the pure inhabitants above "to glorify God," and many are still "on the land of probation," to join in the good work of love and usefulness.

My mother, Mrs. Sarah Levy, died before I knew the love of a mother, but we were left in the care of a loving grandmother, and our father, Mr. John Levy, died in 1861, but we were all grown large enough to care for ourselves.

Our dear grandmother strove the best she knew how to rear us up to be acceptable to all that we may come in contact with, and I bless her name to-day for all she did for me. The mistress, her owner, was of ripe age, with no children, so she took me at an early age to her use and care, being childless. I came in as a good substitute, and being weakly they had to be gentle with me, and I had so much spirit of freedom instilled in me that it was no easy matter to try to subdue it. My inner nature resented any attempt at oppression, so I grew up with a will to do the right and fear no evil, and coming under the direction of the most intelligent class of persons, I emulated their nature and refinement, kept as I was so closely in their association. I can never lose the spirit of fearlessness to do the right. During the civil war I was taken from home by the Mrs. to go up to

---

12. Avery Normal Institute was founded in Charleston on September 12, 1865, with the aid of the American Missionary Association and became a nationally recognized African American educational institution that trained young adults in professional careers and leadership roles for nearly one hundred years. While offering general courses in farming, sewing, cooking, millinery, laundry, housekeeping, etc., Avery also gave its students a classical education, with courses in history, government, economics, languages, literature, teaching methods, natural philosophy, and physiology. In the early 1880s, Avery served as the only educational institution in Charleston that prepared "promising" blacks for college, playing a role in the development of the black professional class. See Edmund L. Drago and Eugene C. Hunt, *A History of Avery Normal Institute from 1865 to 1954* (Charleston: Avery Research Center, 1991); Walter Edgar, *South Carolina: A History* (Columbia: University of South Carolina Press, 1998); and Christine W. Hampton and Rosalee W. Washington, *The History of Lincolnville, South Carolina* (Charleston: BookSurge, 2007).

Anderson C. H.[13] and left my old grandmother behind. As the Federal fleet had commenced to shell the city, so she must leave for safety. And there we were to remain until the war ends. During my absence my dear grandmother died, but the great satisfaction to my sad heart was, she was all right to meet her Lord, and my uncle, a devoted son of hers, was able and would see her body nicely deposited, while her sainted spirit returned to the God that gave it. She left the world without a tear, save for the ones she loved so dear. During my stay at Anderson I was addressed by the architect of the town, who offered himself as a protector for me through life, but I could not see the need of one, since I had a strong arm around me in the person of the kind old lady, acting mistress and mother to me, and I had promised never to leave her alone. She could never bear to have me absent from her in the least. She survived her husband, Mr. John Wilkes, eight years, and I have been her home companion and comfort up to her death. The gentleman, Mr. Cornelius Riley, did not yield to my apology as a refusal, but said "he would wait on time to settle the matter," the mystery of life, follow after me; for the time surely speeded on its wing, and in less than fifteen days from the apology made by me, the time and day came when my support and protector had, in ten days illness, she calmly yielded to the monster—Death. I had the high honor and acceptance of acting as their spiritual helper, and was solicited to make the last prayers for them to hear in life, "as they held true confidence in the knowledge" I had of God and his promises to those who believe on his name. Shortly after, my brother next in age who took me to his arms, died. As this was the time for friends to be known, the gentleman came to my aid, and the necessary time came to accept the protection of the man who after a time became my wedded husband. On the 25th of August, 1854,[14] my pastor, Rev. Farr of the Presbyterian Church being away on vacation, the ceremony was performed by the Rev. Scott Murray of the Baptist Church of this place. I was married in the parlor of Capt. Wm. Henry Perrenneu, in the presence of the white friends and relatives of the old lady

13. Currently called Anderson, South Carolina, the town was originally called Anderson Court House, or C. H., and was granted a post office under that name in 1827.

14. The date would have to be 1864 since she traveled to Anderson and met Cornelius Riley during the war. Moreover, based on the birth date she provides, in 1854 she would have been only fifteen. More likely, she was married the day before her twenty-fifth birthday.

mistress, mother and friend; they were forty in number, the best families of note, viz: the Perrenneus, the Washingtons, the McPhersons, Mileses, the Rev. Keeths family, the Rev. Seabrooks and Gibbes, and the younger part of the families.[15] Yes, surely my colored friends were accorded a place among them, only less in number, but all was as kind as friends could be, with no exceptions. Even their owners were very indulgent in every way and manner. I due all favors and acceptance to all classes of my friends toward me to the "Giver" of the mystery that hangs around my life. I remembered this incident that I deem worthy of note, in revealing the mysterious life and calling. See this: The wife of Lawyer Perreneu Finley of Aiken, S. C., invited the dear old Mrs. to the reception of her nephew who had just returned from college. Their old aunt was not well enough to go out and sent me to represent her. Surely they felt they should please her in her request and sent the coach to convey me to the place. I was met and accepted and was led in to Mrs. Finley who was suffering under a severe attack of illness, and requested that I should hold her place at the end of the table and attend to the young people, and to make it known that they were under the shadow of Mrs. Finley.[16] She had the confidence that I was brave and sufficient to keep and entertain the young people, and I assumed the position with much satisfaction to all, but the task was too taxing to my nerves and after the supper was over and the dancing began I, like Mrs. Finley, failed, and had to call for the coach to take me to the hotel as early as he could. I had an attack of my enemy, a most violent sick headache. I could not partake of any of the dainties. This was at Aiken, S. C. We were boarding at the Swartt's Hotel. So on the next day here comes a man servant bearing a waiter full of nice things for the old lady and myself. This will prove to you that I had said before: how indulged I was by all my friends.

15. *South Carolina Historical and Genealogical Magazine* 39 (1938) notes that in 1863, a Captain W. H. Perroneau assumed command of the one company of the First South Carolina Regiment of Artillery that garrisoned the Castle Pinckney, a small Charleston masonry fortification used as a prisoner-of-war camp and an artillery position during the Civil War. The magazine also lists the Seabrooks as a noted Charleston family, specifically the Rev. Joseph Baynard Seabrook (1809–77).

16. This is perhaps the wife of William Peronneau Finley, president of Charleston College, 1845–57 (now College of Charleston). See Mabel Louise Webber, ed., *SC Historical and Genealogical Magazine: Published Quarterly by the South Carolina Historical Society* (Baltimore: Williams & Wilkins, 1938), 41.

At the close of the war, after the proclamation of liberty to all who were oppressed as slaves of men, my husband moved away for the city of Columbia, S. C., in 1856 [*sic*], and in moving we lost our marriage paper, for there were no regular certificates given in the days of slavery. So, on attending the first annual conference held by this branch of the church, we had Bishop John M. Brown[17] to supply us one, who met us at the boarding house of that good lady friend of mine, Mrs. Polly Pickens,[18] in the presence of Mrs. Rev. James T. Baker, Miss Anna L. Simonds, my adopted, and Judge Wright, then of the Circuit Court of the State of South Carolina, the only negro Judge.[19]

Among the others from here I was carried back to my old birthplace, Charleston, the little "City by the Sea."

From the many calls for my services in places of trust, and seeing my insufficiency, I thought of the words of the great man, Frederick W. Robertson, that

17. Bishop John Mifflin Brown (1817–93) was consecrated as the eleventh bishop of the AME Church and served in that capacity for nearly twenty-five years and in the denomination for nearly sixty. Born in Delaware, little is known of his early life and family, other than that he had an older sister and was raised and provided some education by a Quaker family. He joined the Bethel AME Church in Philadelphia, Pennsylvania, studied barbering, began his training for ministry and rose rapidly in the ranks of church leadership. He helped to establish the AME Church all across the United States, was imprisoned five times for allowing slaves to attend religious services, was instrumental in establishing key educational institutions affiliated with the AME Church, including Allen University and Paul Quinn College, supported the Back to Africa Movement, and was a fierce supporter of the ordination of women. For a complete biographical sketch, see Beverly Bunch-Lyons, "John Mifflin Brown," in *Slavery in the United States: A Social, Political, and Historical Encyclopedia*, ed. Junius P. Rodriguez (ABC-CLIO, 2007), 207–8.

18. Pickens is listed as the defendant in South Carolina Supreme Court case number 1812, *Minton v. Pickens*, 1885. Warren Minton brought this action against Pickens and her husband, Paul, for the partition of a lot of land in the city of Columbia. The complaint was ultimately dismissed.

19. Jonathan Jasper Wright, a native of Lancaster, Pennsylvania, was the first black attorney in the state and the nation's first black judge. He served on the Supreme Court of South Carolina from 1870 to 1877. Wright was a part of the American Missionary Society during Reconstruction and helped to establish schools for illiterate black military personnel. Within a year, he reported that "all of the men could read the New Testament." See Karen Juanita Carillo, *African American History Day by Day: A Reference guide to Events* (Santa Barbara: Greenwood, 2012), 106.

"Education is to unfold nature, to strengthen good, and conquer evil, to give self help to make a man."[20]

O, how burdensome is life devoid of this help, in some degree of its measure.

And with Ruskin, I believe the greatest education "is that directed to make men more thoughtful, merciful and just."[21]

Well, what shall I do? Sick and poor, however, I shall make an effort about the matter. There is a Presbyterian School near me. I shall go there and ask favors of them as one of their branch. The Rev. Adams, pastor of the George Street Church, was President of the School taught by Rev. W. Vauhan as Principal, having the highest grade class under his charge. I fell into his hands, he knowing my aim, done all for me the best he could. The President came in three days of the week, and reviewed our class, which was everything to the anxious pupils, for he was an excellent teacher.

I needed all the help I could get, as I was teaching at the same time a night school for young women and men, who had not the way to attend a day school.

But alas! My husband, not liking Charleston, moved back to Columbia, S. C., much against my profit. However, thank God, I had an exceedingly prosperous season with these fine teachers. And while waiting to hear, shall I stay at school or leave it? I had some very noted persons to call upon me, "desiring me to come to their work as a teacher among their people."

First was the Presiding Elder of the Orangeburg District, R. H. Cain, in behalf of the pastor of the A. M. E. Church at Lewisville, S. C., ninety-two

20. Quoted in *Well-Springs of Wisdom: From the Writings of Frederick W. Robertson*, edited by Rose Porter (Boston: D. Lothrop Company, 1889), 43. Robertson (1816–53) was an Anglican minister, called a "divine," whose sermons were bestsellers when they were published posthumously in 1855. The collections went into multiple editions until the early twentieth century in England, as well as in every English-speaking country in the world, especially the United States. He also believed in universal education and started schools for girls as well as boys. In an era governed by social distinctions based solely on rank, title, and wealth, he preached equal opportunity, with universal education as the way to achieve it.

21. More fully, Ruskin reads, "There is only one cure for public distress, and that is public education, directed to make men thoughtful, merciful, and just." Quoted in *Dictionary of Quotations from Ancient and Modern, English and Foreign Sources*, selected and compiled by Rev. James Wood (London: Frederick Warne and Company, 1899), 476. John Ruskin (1819–1900) was the leading English art critic of the Victorian period; he was also an art patron, draftsman, watercolorist, prominent social thinker, and philanthropist.

miles from Charleston.[22] Then the Rev. Richard Townsend, my former leader, of the Presbyterian Church, for his people at Monck's Corner M. E. Church. And the Rev. Abram Middleton, my father's old friend, and brother to the noted Secretary of the M. E. South Carolina Annual Conference. Rev. James B. Middleton, and the Rev. Charles Manigault, of the M. E. Church at Jacksonville, Fla.

Having partly given the yes to the first man of God, I could but regret I could not be divided, as all these gentlemen were highly thought of by me. I was only waiting my husband's return from Columbia to give the final answer to the acceptance of the Lewisville School, as it was just thirty-eight miles from his place of business.

He consented for me to take the school at Lewisville, now St. Matthew's, S. C., so I sent my word up to the pastor, I shall come when sent for. So they were ready to open the school in October, 1867. They sent earlier than we expected; however, I got my dear young friend, Miss Mary Speissegger, to go up in answer to the call as my companion and assistant, and the Rev. A. G. C. Hamilton[23] will take care of her, until I shall have made all arrangements to leave the city.

I felt blest to have such a friend, as she was one of the sweetest spirits one need wish to have. Bishop John M. Brown remarked to me one day as she was

22. Richard Harvey Cain (1825–87) is mentioned several times in the narrative as a critical component of Riley's spiritual and personal development. Born of free parents in Greenbrier County, Virginia (now West Virginia), the AME preacher was affectionately known as "Daddy Cain" and as a gifted and witty orator. He served two nonconsecutive terms in the United States House of Representatives (1873–75 and 1877–79) during Reconstruction's turbulent years, founded the *South Carolina Leader* in 1866, the newspaper that garnered support for the historic Emanuel AME Church in Charleston, South Carolina, which he pastored for many years after the end of the Civil War, and founded historic Lincolnville, the all-black town for which Riley served as postmistress. In 1880, the AME Church elected Cain to serve as its fourteenth bishop in the Texas-Louisiana Conference. While there, he cofounded Paul Quinn College in Waco, Texas. For a complete discussion of Cain's life and political accomplishments, see "Cain, Richard Harvey," History, Art and Archives, US House of Representatives, http://history.house.gov/People/Detail/10470?ret=True; Eric Foner, *Freedom's Lawmakers: A Directory of Black Officeholders during Reconstruction* (New York: Oxford University Press, 1993), 36; William C. Hine, "Cain, Richard Harvey," in *American National Biography*, vol. 4, edited by Lewis Burnett-Clarke (New York: Oxford University Press, 1999), 188–89.

23. A.J.C. Hamilton, based on a later reference.

advancing toward us: "She is one of the most gentle ladies I have met this side of Baltimore."

I say the truth to tell you. I am a very dependent woman upon my sex for their help in my domestic affairs in life, owing to my poor health, which forbids me ever to be alone, as an attack of illness would take me at night, that demands some help in haste, and the good Lord has, in His own Providential way, made it possible that these helps and comforts are sent to my wants up to the present day.

With their recompense laid to His account, my friend and I should not be termed a bragger. Shall I call her my spiritual child? as through my life and teaching she was brought to know and own her Lord, to the saving of her soul.

In obedience she moved up to answer the demands of the people, and opened the select school. I must close out my private school, much to the regret of parents, pupils and teachers, so as not to have any thing upon my mind to enslave me, but I received a letter to-day, after three weeks absence, from my teacher, sent as follows: "Come at once or I shall close the school and return to the city," for the people say I am "John the Baptist,"[24] and they are in waiting for the greater "answer on next mail."

I thought to trouble the people, and wrote to tell them I am out of money, and waiting on some, but as soon as the news got out, the officers called a meeting and collected the amount needed, and sent it forthwith to my use. So I was compelled to move up in speed.

Let us hear how this will be understood. On my first introduction to the great mind reader, the lamented Bishop Richard Harry Cain, questioned me.

"Sister, are you a Methodist?"

"No, I am Presbyterian."

"O no, you are not, and you shall have to leave your home and go out abroad to learn what you are, and what you are called to be, for I see you are a woman of a great gift, and that position awaits you, but you must go to meet them."

And to test the metal it was put on trial. He called my aid to the funds. Of the building of the great Emanuel A. M. E. Church, Calhoun Street,

24. With the reference to John the Baptist as the forerunner of Christ, Speissegger is seen as the forerunner of Riley in the people's eyes, because they are waiting for the greater preacher.

Charleston, S. C.,[25] I consented to have a sacred tableau, program for two nights, with such scenes as Moses in the bulrushes, Jacob's Twelve Sons, the Sale of Joseph, the Magi's Visit to Bethlehem, etc., and the proceeds to the building fund amounted to one hundred and eighteen dollars ($118), expenses eighteen dollars ($18).

There is the "hand of God," as He works His sovereign will.

Dear Reader, have you forgotten the mysterious vision and revelation in the conversion of the writer? "I am still praising the Name of the Most High for His converting grace."

Now, then, I accepted the lesson as taught us, on this wise: "To accomplish the greater good, one must go where they are most needed." So I have got to

25. The history of the Emanuel AME Church reflects the development of religious institutions for African Americans in Charleston. Similar to the founding of Mother Bethel Church in Philadelphia, Pennsylvania, by Richard Allen and Absalom Jones, Emanuel's roots stem from the organizing of a religious group of free blacks and slaves in 1791 who were then members of Charleston's all-white Methodist Episcopal Church. In 1816, the same year Richard Allen established the first black religious denomination, black members withdrew over disputed burial ground and, under the leadership of Morris Brown, formed a separate congregation under the auspices of the AME Church. In 1822, the church was investigated for its involvement with a planned slave revolt. Denmark Vesey, one of the church's founders, had organized a major slave uprising in Charleston. During the Vesey controversy, the church was burned. Worship services continued after the church was rebuilt until 1834, when all-black churches were outlawed. The congregation subsequently met in secret until 1865, when it was formally reorganized and named Emanuel. The members rebuilt the church in 1872, the building project to which Riley refers as they would have been fundraising in 1867–68. That building was badly damaged in the earthquake of 1886. The current Gothic Revival-style church located on Calhoun Street was built in 1891. Riley writes about attending the dedication of that building and her memories of the earlier structure. Retaining its original altar, communion rail, pews, and light fixtures, the church is one of only a few unaltered religious interiors in Charleston, especially from the Victorian period. Today Emanuel is the oldest AME church in the South and houses the oldest black congregation south of Baltimore, Maryland. The building is one of more than 1,400 historically significant buildings within the Charleston Old and Historic District. The church most recently made history on Wednesday, June 17, 2015, when a young white man entered the church, attended an hour-long Bible study, and then killed nine members of the church, including the pastor, South Carolina State Senator Rev. Clementa Pinkney, the youngest African American elected as a South Carolina state legislator.

the place where the plan of Jehovah called me to be. Having left home through great tribulation, you shall hear it.

As I arrived at the depot on that day, a large number of friends met me, white and colored, with my assistant, and forty school children, who greeted me with welcome to the town. With no less welcome to my dear friend, whom all did learn to love with fervent devotion.

On attending service on the Sabbath, I was presented to the congregation as their teacher in every capacity, in the school, and out of the same, and asked that I might say something as to my desire. Well, I reiterated to them my being in their midst. I am here with you to teach, and to set forth to you and your children the true principles of the Christian, and assured them that I had come to stay. And as they see me to-day, to like me or dislike me, that it will be the same woman, shall I stay with them always? As I have built myself upon the foundation of truth, and there I shall stand as their teacher, even shall the heavens fall, for I believe "God's Word of Promise," that "He shall sustain me," yes, "while He affords me aid, I shall never, never fear," however I may be called to walk through danger, seen or unseen. "His presence will be there."

"Amen. Glory to His Name."

Monday found us in the school house, with seventy-five children in our charge, with the pledge of their parents to help us there, obedience to all the rules of their teacher. Now, as the great work of responsibility was laid out before us, I deem it my duty to the pastor and members of my church in the city to resign my position as teacher in the Sunday School, and informing them that we shall be up here for many months, so far as we can see ahead of time, for when I complained about my boarding place, they set to work and built us a house as comfortable as they could afford, very near the school house, to save us from exposure, and to my satisfaction.

My pastor wrote me the letter, which I shall give you a part to read:

Mrs. C. S. Riley, Select Teacher, Lewisville School, S. C.

My Very Dear Sister—Your very welcome letter I received on my arrival from Florida, where I have been for a few weeks, on a little tour. So I found your letter with a great many others. I am much pressed now to answer them, but I answer yours now among the very first, because I wish to tell you how glad I am that you are able, and have a heart to labor in such a great field and do good, next to preaching the Gospel. I think you have chosen the most useful and blessed avocation in the world. Men may till the soil, that is, honorable and right; they may build houses, and monuments, and cities; but resistless, relentless

Time shall destroy them all, they shall all turn back to their original dust. Not so with him who shapes the immortal mind, makes an impression upon the mind of childhood, but it will last forever—Time cannot efface. There is no power in heaven or earth or hell can wipe it out. As a true teacher, you labor for eternity. Dear Sister, of such kind, faithful and Christian teachers as I believe you and Sister Speissegger to be.

O, you have a good and glorious work. I am so glad to hear of your success. Hold fast to the old faith. But I must close. Give kindest regards to Sister S. When I go to Columbia I will give you a call, if I have the time.

Your Brother in Christ,

BENJAMIN T. JACKSON (White).[26]

Now, we are fully into the work for good. I never gave thought to such a thing as a failure in whatever work I undertake. Did I hear you say the heroes of a battle are laudable? That is to say, "deserving much praise?" A heroine not exempt? "Did you say yes?" *So do I.* Listen, and I shall relate to you of a heroine's victory.

After every arrangement had been completed for the journey to meet the battle I had engaged in, my husband came in and said to me: I just decided in my mind not to have you go to that place. I don't want you among those African Methodists. Well, I stood dumbfounded. While the fire of indignation burned in the soul, almost to its consummation, then I spoke. Why this change? Where is the danger signal? I questioned, and after so much useless words I learned how the change came about. The man who was my leader did not want to lose me from his class, and so taunted my husband to hinder my going, and he meant to disoblige me, to oblige the man. So the war began in earnest, for evil, or for good report.

Now, dear sir, my word is gone up to be their teacher, with your consent, and my word shall ever be my bond, and as much as you are governed by another man to rule me, your honest wife, dear sir, she shall be woman enough to be governed by the conviction of her own mind, and shall die in the attempt to make my promise sure.

26. Riley maintained her membership at the all-white Plymouth Presbyterian Church until 1869, when she officially joined the AME church. Her parenthetical denotation of Benjamin Jackson's race indicates her desire for readers to recognize her affiliation with and admiration by both the black and white religious and social communities.

Now, you let me alone, and if I am wrong, I shall fail in the work, but get out of my way, as I am convicted to be right. As a "child of God," He shall guide me, always in the right.

This he could not deny, as he had seen so much of "God's favor toward me." So he gave up the battle with never to come to see me as to intimidate. So the battle is fought, the victory won, and Zion's field is mine.

"Glory, Hallelujah! Praise the Lord. Amen."

January, 1868, in association with the Rev. Abraham J. C. Hamilton, we had a grand celebration. On the first of January, in memory of the Emancipation Proclamation, teaching our people the gratitude to their Maker in the gift of great men to carry out His purposes.

The school children had a very important part in the exercises of the day, in their recitations, and declarations and songs. Surely the improvement in the old as well as in the young people was marvelous. It did come to pass, "like Ezekiel's dry bones," in the valley "did come together, and lived."[27]

One Mr. Silas McDowal was so enthused, by the little speech of his eight year old son, that he came upon the stand and handed me an envelope containing a two dollar bill, as a token of appreciation.

I taught the six months, five hours daily, and a night school of twenty-five men and women, and the Sabbath School of three hundred, old and young people, with two teachers. We found the work heavy, but not grievous. As some one has truly said, "It is love where e'er the heart is," and my heart was truly in the work. I taught three long years in succession as [*sic*] the select school. We gave no vacation, being controlled by the ambitious power of the mind for my pupils' progress.

Now, dear reader, have you yet accepted the conviction of my friends and admirers, that the life of the writer to their minds is "full of mystery," in character and work, who exemplify to the world "that God deals familiarly with them who love and obey His laws."

I shall like for you to have this event related. Let me begin it. I was presented with a letter, and as I looked to read it, the person robed in white held it up to

27. A reference to Ezekiel 37:1–11. In the passage, the prophet Ezekiel recounts his experience in a valley of dry bones where God commands him to prophesy life and breath to the dismembered remains. Israel, under Babylonian captivity until approximately 600 BC, is figured in the valley as resurrected in the bodies of a great army. The school children's disparate presentations come together for Riley like a great army to participate in the fifth anniversary of the Emancipation Proclamation.

my view, but it was all in Hebrew letters. So I said I have had no learning in this.

"Well," said this stranger, "Figrine, look steady." Then I could make to read "a letter sent by your mother from heaven." "Be ye truthful, and you shall have a legacy." And the letter was hung up over the mantel. Then I awoke out of this mysterious vision. Yes, I related it to my assistant as soon as I came to myself. Now, we agreed to look for its revelation. I see the letter to-day in my mind's eye, just as I saw it then as it was hung up as a reminder. I dare not attempt to picture the bearer, as I cannot, "for it was a spirit." Here here it here comes three strangers to us [*sic*]. He asked to see the principal teacher on important business. So I returned back to the school house where we held a conference together, as to the matter of giving the school over to the charge of the State. Who shall be responsible for the teacher's pay? And concluded the change with pledging the State responsible for tuition due me for three year's services.

Waiting on the poor parents of the children to save enough to pay in the long run, these officers pledged me that the State would pay me at the rate of five cents per day for each child, whose parents had not paid during these years.

Now, the change has come. I am requested to make up my report with the names of the pupils, the day's attendance, their parents' names, and where they dwelt, and what is their reason for not paying. This report must be sent to the Legislature at Columbia, the capital, signed by the School Commissioner and the Senator of the County of Orangeburg, S. C. And in process of law I received an answer to the claim. I received the legacy of a check to be drawn on the State Bank, of thirteen hundred dollars ($1,300).

Say, reader, can you or will you accept my theology as being in secret union with the "divine powers?" Dare you deny such dazzling visions and revelations as the light of God's favor? Say as you will. My legacy was immediately expressed to the Freedman's Bank[28] as a saving investment to coming days of old age, and

---

28. Incorporated by an act of Congress in 1865, the Freedman's Savings and Trust Company (also known as the Freedman's Bank) was established as a banking institution primarily for the benefit of former slaves. Shortly after its creation, two military savings banks at Norfolk, Virginia, and Beaufort, South Carolina, which had been established during the Civil War for savings deposits of African American soldiers, were transferred to the company. The bank established thirty-seven branches in seventeen states and the District of Columbia between 1865 and 1870 and had more than 70,000 depositors and deposits totaling more than $57 million in its nine-year history. While it had no legal connection to it, the Freedman's Bank was morally and practically a part of the Freedman's Bureau and often shared office

infirmity, and with these favors of God towards me, I pledged myself for God to live, and for Him to die, and by God's assisting me I shall be valiant in His cause, and in substance with the poet: "O, help us to help each other Lord, each other's cross to bear, let each a friendly aid afford, and feel his brother's care."[29]

I have lived among the people long enough to learn from observation they were destitute of money as just from the thraldom of slavery they could boast of nothing but their faith in "God's Providential care." The men were all on contract with the owners of the land, and at the end of the year, when the crops were all gathered, and the white man deducted out the poor man indebtedness he is left in debt to begin again for another year, to lose again, with no one to right the wrongs. So he must go on. no one to right the wrongs. So he must go on. [*sic*] Well, I wondered what can be done for him; he must be helped. So I questioned my mind, trusting the "Lord to help me" to find a way to better these conditions. The men were helpless to continue a way. Now I advised them not to go on a contract next year, but to rent from the owner so much land for their own use, and do so much work for the white man per week for the use of the owner's horse, so they arranged to plow three days for the owner and three for himself, with so much for the rent, and in that way they were able to have something to dispose of that would give him a little cash. Then he would take upon the lien of his crop for provisions from the store, and pay in cotton at the

----

space with the bureau, which had also been established in 1865 to supervise and manage "all matters relating to the refugees and freedmen and lands abandoned or seized during the Civil War." See Reginald Washington, *Black Family Research: Records of Post-Civil War Federal Agencies at the National Archives and Records Administration* (Washington, DC: National Archives and Records Administration, 2001), 12–13.

29. Quoted from the third stanza of "Try Us, O God" by Charles Wesley. It was written as a poem in 1742 and then set to music by John B. Dykes in 1875: "Try us, O God, and search the ground Of every sinful heart; Whate'er of sin in us is found, O bid it all depart. / If to the right or left we stray, Leave us not comfortless; But guide our feet into the way Of everlasting peace. / Help us to help each other, Lord, Each other's cross to bear; Let each his friendly aid afford, And feel his brother's care. / Help us to build each other up, Our little stock improve; Increase our faith, confirm our hope, And perfect us in love. / Up unto Thee, our living head, Let us in all things grow, Till Thou hast made us free indeed, And spotless here below. / Then, when the mighty work is wrought, Receive Thy ready bride: Give us in Heaven a happy lot With all the sanctified."

end of the year. In this way about thirty families were able to see their value on the close of the year, and I was able the next season to make arrangements with Mr. Samuel Bennett, Notary of Charleston at the time, and father of the noted Mr. Swinton Bennett, the progressive Notary, now in the firm of Lawrence & Bennett, of Charleston, S. C. Having effected satisfactory arrangements, I shouldered the load; to ship the cotton made by the men on their rented land. As they would bring their cotton, I would meet them at depot, and see them marked for our man, and he would be there to meet the same; and I would go down when notified and receive their money, and purchase by their list such things needed for their family, and bring the division of their part to their gratitude and satisfaction. By using these means the men were led into the way of contriving and arranging for themselves, as all my arrangements were pleasantly and successfully carried out. In all the extra work my schemes were successfully carried on there was no such thing as neglecting, for my rules for order and decorum were strictly carried out by my well-disciplined pupils and my gentle but decided assistant. The Rev. James T. Baker succeeded Rev. Hewitt as pastor, with a wife born to be the helpmate, for it can truly be said she was the life and success to her husband, as the fact stands un-contradicted that many men are in the ministry to-day whose success comes to him through the silent agency of his admirable wife. Such was this highly beloved lady. I found in her a spirit of true love that held us together until the rude hand of death severed, but left me with a hope as "bright as the promise of God" that we shall meet again in that world where death can never enter to part us any more, "Glory Hallelujah, praise the Lord!" "The harvest is so great, and the laborers so few,"[30] I was pressed to do much work in the church to help the pastor. Just before Rev. Hamilton's work closed, he had a grand three days' meeting, from Friday until Sunday. Bishop R. H. Cain was our P. E.[31] at that time. Not being able to be with the Rev. Hamilton on Sunday, he sent up to his help a visiting preacher, a fine scholar. He gave us a fine discourse at 11 a. m. and returned to the city to preach at night at the great Emanuel Church, and to think, the preacher, Hamilton, left his people at the last of the feast and followed the

30. A reference to Matthew 9:37: "Then saith he unto his disciples, The harvest truly is plenteous, but the labourers are few; Pray ye therefore the Lord of the harvest, that he will send forth labourers into his harvest."
31. Presiding Elder.

preacher to the city. All cried "Shame!" for him, and going to the city where he had to pass by the church ground where the meeting was held, and on passing he flung out a note to the deacon of the church to solicit me to call for all those parties interested in their salvation "and record their names for him." But the people were all discouraged in the act of the preacher and were preparing to leave the ground. I declined doing so, but the local elders and deacon constrained me to aid them to carry on the work, and I said I would try. So the alarm was sounded out by these honorable Godly men, "Hear, hear, the teacher is going to speak!" and there was an immediate halt, and in a short time the ground was packed with anxious hearers. Then I selected the 349 Hymn, "Sinners, the Voice of God, his Mercies Speak To-day."[32] The hymn was sung by the whole people in one of the old Methodist tunes, that is "Merit to Awaken the Jonahs out of Sleep."[33] As in a maze, not knowing how to meet the anxious and critical ear and hearts, I began by saying, Your pastor begged me to take the names of all who desire to gain "the Church as the Door which leads to the Way of God." At this point I saw the danger of the sinners in delaying, or denying the invitation, and as though overshadowed I came out of fear and doubt, "and God helping me," I made an alarming appeal for the unsaved to accept the terms of "the glorious Gospel of God's only Son" that aroused the meeting to a fever heat of the "Spirit that burns into the soul" to the consuming of sin which resulted in seventy-eight accessions to the army of the A. M. E. connection, and at the night meeting sixty more were added, giving a total gain from Satan's camp "over into the army of the Lord" of one hundred and thirty-eight, with the most of them claiming "the new birth in Christ." Some of these are in Glory now, while others are still with me in the wilderness journey, seeking the city that lieth at the end of our voyage, "whose builder and maker is

32. "Sinners, the Voice of God, Regard," words by John Fawcett (1782) and music by John B. Calkin (1875).

33. Although no reference for "Merit to Awaken the Jonahs out of Sleep" is available, it is likely that most of the hymns Riley would have sung and to which she refers come from *A Collection of Hymns, for the Use of the Methodist Episcopal Church, Principally from the Collection of the Rev. John Wesley, A. M. Late Fellow of Lincoln College, Oxford*, revised and corrected, with a supplement (New York: George Lane and P. P. Sanford, 1840). The hymnal is about 3.5 inches by 2.5 inches by 1.5 inches. The AME Church has always used the ME Church hymnbook, even today.

God."[34] You shall find me at any time you may desire to see me, on the grand old regular march, though but an "Armor-bearer I may be. If in the battle to my trust I'm true, mine shall be the honors in the grand review."[35] This is the beginning of the revelation of the Mysterious Life and calling of the writer. Now let "the name of God have all the glory." We have in the preceding letter the expression of our present Bishop John M. Brown, his opinion of the ability of the writer to act in all capacities. Let us read it.

Baltimore, Sept. 22, 1869.

DEAR MADAM:

Bishop Brown particularly requested me to send you some of the circulars for the National Labor Convention. You shall see its great importance at this stage of our history in the United States. By it we hope to so organize our labor so as to make it permanent and respectable, and unless there is some general system inaugurated, colored labor in the Southern States will be as it is in the Northern States, at the mercy of white combination.

Now we want you to call together some of the live men of your State and let them call a big meeting and elect your delegates to meet the Columbia Convention. Let them pass resolutions and have it published in your daily paper. "Do this and we have a hope; do it not and we live without a hope." Let me hear your determination.

Yours truly,

ISAAC MEYERS,[36]
Box 522, Baltimore, Md.

34. A reference to Hebrews 11:8–10: "By faith Abraham, when he was called to go out into a place which he should after receive for an inheritance, obeyed; and he went out, not knowing whither he went. By faith he sojourned in the land of promise, as in a strange country, dwelling in tabernacles with Isaac and Jacob, the heirs with him of the same promise: For he looked for a city which hath foundations, whose builder and maker is God."

35. Taken from the hymn "Only An Armor Bearer," by Philip B. Bliss (1838–76): "Only an armor bearer, yet may I share / Glory immortal, and a bright crown wear; / If in the battle to my trust I'm true, / Mine shall be the honors in the Grand Review." The hymnal does not provide a date for the song, but given his birth and death dates, Bliss was Riley's contemporary. He was born in Pennsylvania, died in a train wreck in Ohio at the age of thirty-eight, and was a prolific song-writer and singer who wrote over sixty hymns.

36. Isaac Myers (1835–91) was an African American labor leader from Baltimore,

Yes, indeed, the meeting was called, aided by the pastor, Rev. James Baker and the officers of the church and all our county officers, and on the 29th day of October we had a stage erected on the school campus, decorated by the ladies' busy hands, and the writer directing it, and to her pride fifteen hundred men answered to the call. Addresses were made, resolutions were passed, delegates elected, and sufficient collected to meet the expenses of the delegate. Mysterious, indeed. We had a grand and enjoyable day long to be remembered, but O, how sad a change a week may bring to us. Truly says the wise Solomon: "Life is but vanity and vexation of spirit."[37] Sad news to tell you, my friend and associate is ill with a fever. I have called to her aid one of the most skillful physicians in the place. A week has passed and left us with no improvement in her case but she calls me to her bedside. I hasten. "What will you have me do, dearest?" I "called you to let you know that I am going home to my reward, and I must leave you." "O, no; you are not going to leave me now, will you?" "Yes, my dear friend, my work is done, but yours has just now begun. There is a great

---

Maryland. Born to free parents, Myers, an entrepreneur, worked as a ship caulker, porter, and shipping clerk. He apprenticed with a leading black ship caulker and by the age of twenty became a supervisor, "caulking some of Baltimore's largest clipper ships." In response to racist practices by white ship caulkers, Myers began his work as a labor organizer, serving as president of Baltimore's Colored Caulkers' Trades Union Society and later as president of the Colored National Labor Union (CNLU). The Colored National Labor Convention was held in Washington, DC, December 6–10, 1869. In preparation for the convention, Bishop Brown instructed Riley to elect delegates at the upcoming October, Columbia, South Carolina, AME convention. Fifteen-hundred men answered the request. They were able to elect delegates and raise money to send them to the December CNLU convention. The US National Archives and Records Administration notes that African Americans participated in labor actions as early as 1835. After the Civil War, newly freed people participated in numerous labor organizations as well. For information on Myers, see "Isaac Myers: In the Business of Leadership," Maryland State Archives, http://msa.maryland.gov/msa/stagser/s1259/121/6050/html/imyers.html. See also John Curl, *For All the People: Uncovering the Hidden History of Cooperation, Cooperative Movements, and Communalism in America* (Oakland, CA: PM Press, 2012), 68; James Gilbert Cassedy, "African Americans and the American Labor Movement," *Prologue Magazine* 29 no. 2 (Summer 1997), http://www.archives.gov/publications/prologue/1997/summer/american-labor-movement.html; for an image of the convention proceedings, see http://sceti.library.upenn.edu/sceti/printedbooksNew/index.cfm?TextID=77925_0&PagePosition=1.

37. This theme is repeated by Solomon in the book of Ecclesiastes, for example, 1:14, 2:11, and 6:9.

work laid out for you to do; 'you just be true to your faith in God' and He will be with you in all your labors and toil, and 'when you shall have fulfilled God's designs' He shall call you home, and we shall meet to part no more. 'I am safely passing through the cleansing blood of Jesus to be presented to His Father, God.' Let me hear your voice in prayer as I am leaving the shore of time." Thanks to God, I had been able to stand the serious ordeal, and granted her desire. Can we not see God in His providential arrangements for His people? Just before she yielded to death, she pleaded to God in prayer to send a dear friend of hers to be with me, and then said to me, "God is going to send you my young friend to be with you. You must love her as your daughter, because I loved her and I know she will love you as a mother, for the love she has for me." Sure I promised to love her for all I could. Now do you think she prayed in vain? No, indeed. On a week before she died this friend of hers came up to assist in nursing her in the person of Miss Anna L. Simonds, and to direct her burial arrangements. She also so arranged her affairs at home to the satisfaction of all and complied with her sainted friend's request of her, and I am thankful to tell you, dear reader, she has filled every space as was hoped for by her lamented friend, and no child of my own could be more true and good to a mother than this, my adopted daughter, Anna, who is and has been ever since we first met, my sole companion and help in and under all circumstances in life. So I was never in want of a true friend and help. In the school house she was just to my aid and in every other work and way. We have for our P. E. this year the excellent and pure principled young Christian, M. B. Salter,[38] now Bishop, who was of much help to me. As he came to meet his conference, he would visit the school, as an appreciator of its value and the good it has and is doing. The greatest feature of his coming was to have devoted to sacred service one hour each morning to the delight of the young people in the hope of their spiritual benefit.

Rev. Erasmus Henry Gourdine is now our pastor. He met me at my post of duty and as usual interested in the church. He was told of this by the people,

---

38. Moses Benjamin Salter (1841–1913), the twenty-first bishop of the AME Church, was born in Charleston, South Carolina, converted to Methodism, and joined the AME Church at sixteen. He was licensed to preach in 1865, pastored some of the largest AME churches in South Carolina and Georgia, and was known as "an able preacher of the evangelistic type." He was elected bishop in 1892 and served both South Carolina and Florida. From 1892 to 1896, he served as the president of the Board of Trustees of Allen University in Columbia, South Carolina. See *AME Church Review* 9, no. 2.

more than he had as yet seen, the confidence of his people in my work, constrained him to call on me and solicit my associating "with him in the work of
the Lord," and that I should consent to whatever work or position the church
should call upon me to fulfill. Well, I could hardly object to it, as my inner life
was enveloped in the promises "to spend and be spent" "for the glory of God
and the progress of his cause." You can see at once how I became a "preacher
of the Word." I was at this time a member of the Plymouth Church, but considering the large field of labor before me, and the "talent or gift to be put out
to usury,"[39] I accepted, to do as he requested of me, and thought not what of
the position I may be called to fill; however my "yes" has gone out of my mouth
not to return void, so I joined my name in the number as a full member of one
of the grandest negro organizations known among the race. This strong association is here to be seen as made in the rapid progress in the present year of its
age and now sweeping over every obstruction in its way. Yes, "Glory Hallelujah,
praise the Lord!"

Here comes the Rev. "Good morning, Sister Riley." "Praise the Lord,
brother, I am up to-day." I come to inform you that you were appointed in the
Leaders' board last night a Leader of Class No. one, a class of elderly ladies, in
persons of the Preacher Hazel's wife, an excellent Christian lady, with Mrs.
Prioleau[40] and Mrs. Huldy Miller, all of fine metal. "The good Lord chooses
always to meet with us," and a glorious time was always ours. This at once
brought to my mind in fresh recollection of the prediction of the sainted and
lamented Bishop Cain, viz.: "You will never need seek position or honors, sister,
for they shall always come to you." So you see as well as I "that the words of
this wise prophet of his day" were not spoken at random. We shall note the
work as the days go by. I shall be solely dependent, however, on memory, as
singular enough to say, I have kept no diary. So I am writing up, as pressed to
do, this little book from the memory of fifty-two years back, leaving out six
years of childhood, with witnesses of these facts as written are alive and are my
associates. You promised with us to note the days as they come and go. Well,
here is another demand of the church. A month has passed. The Rev. Pastor
comes again with news from the Board. Well, sister, the brethren have decided

39. A reference to Jesus's parable of the talents or parable of the ten pounds: Matthew
25:14–30 and Luke 19:12–27.

40. Susan Prioleau, the wife of the Rev. Lewis S. Prioleau, pastor of St. Matthews AME
Church in South Carolina, and the mother of George Washington Prioleau (see note 71).

to offer you the quarterly meeting for local orders, as it was put to all the churches in the circuit, have voted their pleasure in the same. They gave me no voice in the matter, but I dared not murmur, as I had consented that they should use me as the church saw fit, but silently rejoiced to find my life so useful to "the work of the Gospel and the Advancing of the Redeemer's kingdom."

The quarterly conference was held seven miles from the old mother church, Bethel,[41] where I taught my school. I could not attend the meeting on Saturday, not being well, so I was presented in my absence to the good Presiding Elder, Hiram Young, for Local Preacher's License, and universally accepted by the Conference, and on Sabbath morning the local deacon was sent to convey me to the service of the day, and to be confirmed by the Elder. So daughter and myself arranged ourselves and we arrived in time to hear the discourse of the Elder. After closing his instructive, soul-searching service, he announced, without notifying me, that preaching again at three o'clock by our sister, C. S. Riley, and avoided me, that no apology could be had. However I obeyed, and did the best I could. Be ye assured we had an additional number as a woman was to preach. "God being with me," I ascended to the work, and used the 46th Psalm, 1st verse: "God is our refuge and strength, a present help in time of trouble." At the close of my weak yet earnest effort in setting forth the "Safety of God's people" under so great a defender, so strong a protector, sixteen souls came forward and joined in the army of the "Lord on the terms of the Gospel." Two of the number claimed to be converted and became strong and useful men and valiant for the Master's cause. With believers renewing their pledge to stay in the army "of the Lord, until the war is ended, God helping them," we sing "Glory and Praise to Jesus give for his Redeeming Grace."[42]

At the South Carolina Conference, held in Columbia, S. C., in 1871, where I, with Miss Emily Rodeny, was offered to the conference and recommended by the lamented Bishop R. H. Cain, then our Presiding Elder, some wrote me to come up to the same as my name was used in my absence and I hurried up to the seat of the conference just in time to hear the report as it was read by the secretary, as follows: The two ladies, Miss E. A. Rodney and Mrs. C. S. Riley,

41. Bethel AME Church in Columbia, South Carolina, is still in existence at 921 Woodrow Street.

42. From the hymn "And Are We Yet Alive?" by Charles Wesley (1844): "And are we yet alive, / And see each other's face? / Glory and thanks to Jesus give/For His almighty grace!"

are elected life members of the Missionary Society in consideration of their earnest, faithful and efficient labors as missionaries.[43] On motion of Rev. Sowney Hazel, each preacher was requested to contribute fifty cents in honor of the missionary ladies to our ranks, and the snug little sum of fifty dollars was added to the treasury. The Rev. B. T. Tanner, now Bishop Tanner, was elected at the same time honorary member of the same.[44] He was then invited to address the meeting, and did so in his own masterly manner, and this is the way the calls come, and bring its honors after it. We learn in Holy Writ that the women of old were also honored by "the Blessed Master for their faithfulness toward him." Did he not leave it on record in the Holy Book that whenever that book is read that the name of these women shall be mentioned as a memorial of their good works? And these accepted times in the Gospel is the incentive principle of my devotion to "the honor of God's name."

On returning to the duties of my school, I met everything in order. The duties of the same were carried on by my helper and daughter, Anna, and the trustees of the school gave the highest appreciation of my service and discipline of the school, the Commissioner not exempted—purchased by a life consecrated to the work. Well, what now? Who are to bear the blunt of criticism? Who, I? O, no. Indeed you would not be so cruel to the woman for preaching the simple Word of God? Well, here comes the "Man of God." Dear sister, I have a special call away for a week on important business, and with the full consent of the officers I should like to leave the church under your care. The brethren are all with you. You will also be with the brethren in their board

43. The two women are listed in the 1879 roll of members of the Columbia, South Carolina, conference as female missionaries, the only two women listed.

44. Benjamin Tucker Tanner (1835–1923) was the father of the acclaimed artist Henry Ossawa Tanner (1859–1937) and Halle Tanner Dillon Johnson (1864–1901), the nation's first black woman physician and the first woman of any race to practice medicine in the state of Alabama. Bishop Tanner was born in Pittsburgh, Pennsylvania, and educated at Avery College and Western Theological Seminary, both in Allegheny City, Pennsylvania. He later earned a doctorate of divinity at Wilberforce College in Wilberforce, Ohio. He founded an AME church and the nation's first school for freedmen, both in Washington, DC, and later became editor of *The Christian Recorder*, the publication arm of the AME Church. He was the author of several books, including *An Apology for African Methodism* (1867) and *Outline and Government of the A.M.E. Church* (1883). For more on Tanner, see William Seraile, *Fire in His Heart: Bishop Benjamin Tucker Tanner and the A.M.E. Church* (Knoxville: University of Tennessee Press, 1999).

meeting and give all needed advice. You are appointed to preach for me on Sunday and I did all I could to show the pleasure of "the good Lord in our work." We also held the Board on Monday evening. We had the best report rendered in that had been for some time past. I think the Sabbath services aided greatly to its success for we had a good day of it, "the Lord was in his holy temple, and all the people were silent before him." They seemed not to have seen the gender of the speaker, but was solely arrested by "the words of God," taken from John 12: 7— "Then said Jesus: Let the woman alone." Jesus, the true friend of the helpless, and their strength in weakness, a sure defense in time of need. "Glory be to God."

All is right with the people and their woman preacher, the pastor is at his post again. We are preparing to leave for the annual conference at Newberry, Feb., 1872, Bishop Brown, our Presiding Elder in the chair. During the hour for motions and resolutions, the Rev. Felix H. Torence made the motion that Sister C. S. Riley be appointed to the agency of the Payne Institution at Cokesbury, S. C. The conference took it in readily and voted it with great animation, and the Bishop signed me licensed for the same with the request that the pastors welcoming and encouraging me in the use of their pulpit and aid.[45] So I did as much for the school in my travel during the year that my poor health and school work allowed me. However I was able at the sitting of the next conference to render in my report as follows:

Dear Bishop and Brethren of the Columbia, S. C., Conference, and
    Trustees of the Payne Institute:

    Your agent begs to make the following report of moneys collected from the various pastors and churches:

Ladies of Lincolnville . . . . $ 9.00
Rev. G. W. Prioleau, Double Spring 5.00
Rev. F. J. Youngs, Player's Cross Road 7.00
Rev. A. E. Gregory, Mayesville Circuit 7.00

45. According to the conference records, the conference met in Sumter in January 1872 and Newberry in 1874. Unfortunately, Riley's appointment to the Payne Institution at Cokesbury as one of the school's earliest principals is not recorded in either set of minutes. The Payne Institute was founded by the AME Church in Cokesbury, South Carolina, in 1870 to educate newly freed black people. Ten years later, because of racial violence, the school was moved to Columbia, South Carolina, and renamed Allen University.

Rev. James White, St. Paul's Mission 4.00
G. G. W. Edmonds 8.00
Rev. P. M. Hartwell, Bishopville 8.00
Rev. S. Williams, High Hill Mission 5.00
Collected from individuals 1.40
                                                                              _____

Total collected $54.90
Traveling expenses $22.25
Commission 12.50
                                                              _____

In hand $20.15
           Respectfully submitted,

                                                    C. S. RILEY.

So every year brings its changes to our sadness or our joys, as the case may be. It was a sad day when the news reached around that one of our leading men, viz: B. F. Randolph, Esq.,[46] was called to the door of the car at the Hodges depot and deliberately shot dead by the heathen white man, for the teaching of his people. He was returning to the city from a large gathering where he had been invited to address his people. This heathenish act of prejudice against intelligence, for he was highly so, caused the interest in the Payne Institute to grow less each term, as of a necessity one must pass through this station to reach Cokesbury, and parents felt the place unsafe for the young students.

This caused serious consideration to have the school carried to some better point, so Columbia was chosen after a few years, and the new name Allen University.

46. Benjamin Franklin Randolph (1820–68) was an outspoken Reconstruction-era political leader, educator, and AME minister who was born in Kentucky, educated in Ohio at Oberlin College and Seminary, and served in South Carolina. Born free to parents of mixed ethnicity, Randolph served as a US Army chaplain during the Civil War and later worked with the newly formed Freedman's Bureau as a teacher and its assistant superintendent of schools in South Carolina. He worked as a party organizer when the Republican Party began formally organizing in South Carolina in 1867 and was elected a year later as a state senator. That same year, while he was canvassing for the Republican Party, he was shot and killed, according to most reports, by the Ku Klux Klan. For more on Randolph, see Bernard E. Powers Jr., *Black Charlestonians: A Social History, 1822–1885* (Fayetteville: University of Arkansas Press, 1994), 89, 149, 230; and Foner, *Freedom's Lawmakers*, 175–76.

The labors of the school of one hundred and forty-three pupils, and the urgent demands of the church, had so prostrated me, that I was made quite ill, and after being convalescent, the agency had to be abandoned for a time, yet I did much at home.

Bishop J. B. Campbell[47] succeeded Bishop Brown for the next four years, and he saw fit, through the recommendation of Elder William M. Thomas, licensed me to the agency for the church being built by my sister and colleague, now Mrs. Emily Rodney Williams, known as Williams' Mission, with the understanding to canvass for the same as I can.

In considering my feebleness at this time, during the dear Bishop's visits in the district, I had the pleasure of entertaining him, with his dear estimable wife. So the Elder took the Bishop to St. George's, and left his wife in my care in his absence. Elder Thomas thought, however, an appointment was out for me to serve, but as he had the Bishop, it would cover all the ground, but they were in waiting for the woman preacher, and that was all in it.

The Bishop returned the next day, and said to me: "Get ready, sister, and go down to those people," for at the approach of the train they left the church and

47. Jabez Pitt Campbell (1815–91) was the eighth bishop consecrated in the AME Church, in 1864. His early life was fraught with challenges; although he was born free, he was promised as "collateral security" for his father's debt to a Captain Pierce. To avoid being sold, he ran away at age thirteen to his mother, who was living in Philadelphia, and was then bound in servitude to a tailor. He fulfilled his obligation at the age of seventeen and gained his independence. In Philadelphia, he joined the Bethel AME Church and received his license to exhort in 1837, thus beginning his itinerant preaching career. He was licensed to preach in 1839 and ordained in 1843. He served appointments in New England, New York, Maryland, and Pennsylvania, during which time he served as the editor and general book steward of *The Christian Recorder*, from 1856 to 1860. He was the first AME bishop to visit California and organized both the California and Louisiana Conferences. According to Jessie Carney Smith, *Notable Black American Women* (2:80), he also founded the Ocean Grove Conference, known as an Annual Missionary Jubilee, a type of religious holiday: "Bishops from New York and Philadelphia met with local authorities and the Pennsylvania Railroad to coordinate special excursion trains for celebrants, singers, and bands who came together for several days of evangelism." He was married to Mary Ann Shire Campbell, a noted philanthropist and community and church worker. She was also close friends with the social reformer, writer, and educator Gertrude E. H. Bustill Mossell (1855–1948). The Campbells were widely known for their charitable work in Philadelphia. For a complete biographical sketch written by Fannie Jackson Coppin, the wife of Bishop Levi Coppin, see Fannie Jackson Coppin, "In Memory of Bishop Jabez Pitt Campbell," *A.M.E. Church Review* 8, no. 2 (October 1891): 152–53.

ran a half mile to meet the missionary, to "gallant her up to the church." And on
my leaving this morning the Elder begged me to send you down, and I promised
to do so. "Go, my sister, and preach with the authority of your Bishop."

In obedience I left the Bishop and his wife in the hands of my careful and
capable daughter, and the pastor's family. I arrived in time for evening service.
I exhorted the assembly "On the mystery of God's goodness and mercy to
sinners," and the result was seen at the close of our effort, for the Elder was
with me, and the people demonstrated "the Presence of God."

Among them many were "blest, to be saved through Christ our Lord." The
people became unmanageable in the demonstration of the spirit of love, that
the elder and your sister were in danger of being pressed to injury, and the
officers had to steal me out from the congregation, and lock us in the parsonage,
and guard the door from the happy people.

These were common events at meetings of this kind in former times, but we
question now, "where is the faith you once had in the Word of God?" Who
distinguished [*sic*][48] "the fire of the Spirit?" Who amended the old time religion
you used to call the Benjamin Mess and the Jeremiah Fire?"[49] "Yes, we see it
sometimes in an unrecognized flame."

These services ought to commence the objections to the elevation of the
woman. The murmuring after woman. Equality, however, means good. She
may be able to accomplish, than these, the hindrance of "the advancement of
God's Kingdom," by "their zeal with no gift."

Not "so with the good man," Elder William Thomas. He understands "the
Divine Maker of man is no respecter of persons," so "He calls whom He wills,
and chooses whom He wants."

After this meeting I had an immediate call to Sumter, S. C., by the lamented Rev. James White. I stopped over and preached at Mount Pisgah for
Rev. Silas Jefferson. "We took in seven in the church to serve the Lord." The
next day, Sunday, I went to Rev. White's work, and preached for his people,
from Exodus 20: 5. Many believed and were saved.

I left Monday for the school work, and on arriving found everything in
order, kept so by my daughter and assistant. I remained at this work the month
out, and was now prepared to supply the churches calling me. According to the

48. Extinguished.

49. "Benjamin Mess" is an old reference to a greater portion of the Holy Spirit from
Genesis 43:34; "Jeremiah Fire" is a reference to Jeremiah 20:9 and 23:29.

promise of the pastor to help, I made a start for help at the Mother Church, the old Emanuel, Charleston, S. C. The Rev. N. B. Sterrett,[50] the strong, successful man of the army, collected for my help the sum of fifteen dollars.

Here I am now at Littleton, with Rev. D. S. Rice, the Moses stamp in spirit. I am out for the aid of Orangeburg Mission Church. Emanuel started me out with her aid of fifteen dollars.

Through the call of the Rev. N. B. Sterrett, D. D.	$15.00
Preached for Rev. Rice, ten accession with	3.15
At Winnsboro, Rev. C. S. Goasley, D. D., fifteen accession with	4.90
Then at White Hall, Rev. Harrison Williams ten accession and collected	2.95
To Jonesville we collected	2.00
Then to Newberry ten accession and collected	4.90
To Spartanburg three accession, collected	3.00
And to Union, Dr. B. F. Porter, pastor, six accession, collected	6.00
And to Barnwell, Rev. Israel McGowan, five accession	10.00

Rev. Rice took to Clowney Gin House,[51] as we had no church, and the master man loaned the employed hands the empty barn. Well, it was packed when we got there, and it was quite amusing to see the men climbing to seats on the beam of the loft. You are led to believe this was a rough crowd, but to the contrary they were surprisingly awed by the woman preaching, and spellbound to the close of the meeting.

Twenty-two accession for Rev. Rice's Mission and collected	$4.20
Preached next for Rev. William Lites, thirteen accession, collected	5.00
Then to Rev. Lattie, Fairfield, twelve accession	1.50

This closes my month's work. I am on my return to school work. You see how indulged I am by parents and trustees, for my labors in all departments, but the school goes on just the same in my absence, with my aids.

50. Rev. Norman B. Sterrett was the founder and first Pastor of Mt. Zion AME Church in Charleston, South Carolina, from 1882 to 1884. The church, located at 5 Glebe Street, is still in existence.

51. Engine house; a structure to enclose a horse mill or cotton gin.

I may give you, my readers, some of the incidents met with in my travels. After preaching at "one of the churches" of Rev. Grimes, white, a man followed so close behind me, to my discomfort. I called the Reverend's attention to it, who questioned his action. Oh, nothing, sir, I was just looking to see "is she a real woman or an angel," but it was proved that my fur capes were not wings, and that I was flesh and blood.

He came up and shook my hand, and said: "God bless your soul," and left the church saying: "The world is coming to an end, for I never seen this before, but I see it to-night."

At another church a sister came up to speak with me, and said to me, the white lady I work for told me to "look at your fingers and see is you a real woman." Then I asked her: "Well, sister, are you satisfied?" I thought her instructor was a very poor Bible reader, or not a Bible reader at all, or she may have learned from the truth it contains therein, "That God's ways of doing is not as man's ways." It is too far above the finite mind, "the mystery of His power in moving among His creatures."

Bishop Brown is again our Bishop, and having had the promise of the members of Cokesbury Church to contribute to the help of the school "during his official visit to the work," and was not able to return, he wrote to inform them that he would send me to collect, and after receiving orders from the Bishop, and the list of the members' names who promised their contributions, and having a call to attend the annual camp meeting in Abbeville District, I thought to make it all in one route. So I started for the camp meeting, where I was slated for the three o'clock service, and to leave on Monday to meet the appointment at Cokesbury, having to serve at three P. M.

I met it in a pouring rain, the dampness of the stand being much against my health. I found myself suffering from the dampness the next day, with a fearful cold. I left, however, for to meet my appointment at Cokesbury. I arrived there at 12 M., but I grew very sick, and by night my throat was nearly closed. I could not dare to leave the bed, so I sent for the principal of the school, Prof. G. W. Morris, and solicited his aid to collect the amount, as noted on the Bishop's list, and inform the church of my illness, and to my great satisfaction, and the praise of the people, they sent me the cash amount of thirteen dollars.

"Praise God for the Gospel," that make men true to their trust.

Sad for me I had to have the doctor called in the next day, Dr. John Garry, brother to C. M. Garry, who had me all right in a few days, to renew my journey. All but an attack of erysipelas[52] in the right eye that he gave me a remedy

---

52. Bacterial skin infection that occurs on the face and is treated with antibiotics.

for, and he kindly gave me a list of doctors that I may call on should I need attention to be treated, on the merits of his name.

He had his wife to send me the Abbeville Medium, with the report of the camp meeting. He thought I should see the piece and save it, and so I did. I thank the doctor very much for the acknowledgment and kindness shown to the A. M. E. Church through their humble missionary. I was truly proud of the report, that read as follows:

"COLORED CHRISTIANS IN CAMP."

The annual camp meeting at Tabernacle began on last Wednesday, and closed to-day, after the usual succession of exciting sermons and hopeful conditions. There was a large attendance during the entire meeting, under all the unfavorable conditions of the wind and weather.

Rev. H. B. Presley was in charge, being aided by a number of visiting clergymen from abroad. Three or four services were held daily. There was much zeal and earnestness shown by those who attended.

On Sunday extra excursion trains were run from all intermediate points. There were on the ground, on Sunday, twenty-five hundred persons. Had the weather allowed they would have had twice that number.

Four sermons were delivered during the day, but the most striking feature of the day's doings was the sermon of Sister C. S. Riley, a colored woman, traveling by special permission of the Bishop of the church, "in behalf of the Payne Institute, at Cokesbury, S. C."

She preached from John xix: 5 — "Behold the Man" — and kept the attention of her hearers, both white and colored, to the close of her discourse. The sermon was the best preached during the day, and had considerable merit in it. "It was good Gospel" all the way through, and set the congregation all a shouting.

We have not heard the exact number of conversions, but the Spirit seemed to be at work on Sunday, and numbers of the overjoyous ones went into a trance and were carried out to their tents.[53]

Now, dear reader, you see the result of the woman "preaching Christ, with Christ, to the glory of His Name. Amen. Amen."

53. Dr. John Garry was likely white, for Riley thanks him for his kindness shown to the AME Church. Moreover, the *Abbeville Medium* titles the article "Colored Christians in Camp." The notation of race indicates that the writer and potential readers are not likely black. The article notes Riley's sermon as one of the most striking. The *Abbeville Medium* was a semiweekly newspaper that was published from 1871 to 1923.

I left Cokesbury for Laurens County, accompanied by my daughter Anna, to the Rev. Isaac Grant, pastor and manager of a very noted camp meeting of two weeks session, made from the fact that a woman would preach at eleven o'clock on the first Sabbath of the meeting.

The meeting commencing truly on Thursday previous, and for a purpose, the pastor wrote me not to appear until the next week ending. The people were then kept under an exciting expectation looking for her to enter the camp on any day, and "may ascend the platform." And they being absent, so the rush was made every day. They dare not gaze upon the scene "their eyes longeth to behold."

I served the Rev. Robert Sutliff in the same District until the day "we were to make our debut." You should have heard what a demonstration of joy at my arrival. Some of the sisters shouted for joy at the reality of my presence. I spoke in my soul the 103rd Psalm: "O, bless the Lord, my soul, and forget not all of His benefits."

The camp meeting held its own—an increase every day. I was held in reserve for the eleven o'clock service. So the multitude was attracted, and seemed to enjoy the very presence of the woman that was to preach on Sunday. They seemed to regard her as a monument of God's mysterious work. These acts of their's brought me to deliberate on the fact that since "Christianity is received by the world woman is created a new race," says Beecher.[54] And once "she is made equal to man, becomes his superior."[55]

I am with Socrates.

I did not create these grand expressions, but I am fully in accordance with these "persons of superior minds."

Bowe says: "Next to God, men are indebted to woman. First, for life itself, then for making that life itself worth having."[56]

On Sabbath, at twelve, God's chosen instrument arose "with a smothering multitude of eager minds" to be satisfied, and the Bread of Life was selected

54. Henry Ward Beecher, the brother of the abolitionist writer Harriet Beecher Stowe. The actual line is "Women are a new race, recreated since the world received Christianity." Quoted in Henry Ward Beecher, *Star Papers: Or, Experiences of Art and Nature* (Bedford, MA: Applewood Books, 1855), 71.

55. Attributed to Socrates: "Once made equal to man, woman becomes his superior."

56. Bowe is actually Christian Nestell Bovee (1820–1904), an American author and lawyer: "Next to God, we are indebted to women, first for life itself, and then for making it worth having."

from Luke 5: 20—"And the people were amazed and filled with fear, and said we have seen strange things to-day."[57]

All we can say about the result of the message is that "Elijah's God was with us, who answers by fire."[58] There was a man in the assembly, a leader of the church, who had fallen from grace, and caused many who were led by him, to do the same. This man was convinced of his wrong, and arose in the congregation and acknowledged to the church his wrongs, and returned to God and his Christ on that memorable Sabbath day, and was saved.

"Glory, Hallelujah! Praise the Lord! Saved in the Blood of the Lamb!"

It was then announced that the missionary will close the meeting on Thursday, at 12 M., with a very serious and mysterious service, having been requested of an old "Mother of the Church," bordering her century, the mother of several stalwart sons, who consented to the singular request, that the "monument of God's favor should preach her funeral, as "she shall never see me again in this world."

"Now, how shall you reason out this, dear reader?" With the mysterious life and calling? Well, I consented to preach the sermon of the "dead, yet living." It is not surprising that the unique service of this great and last day drew the estimated three thousand people. The Rev. Grant said to me:

"Sister, they have you in a close place."

"No," said I, "you just gaze on her Christian life and labors, as I am well acquainted with the way and manner of her acceptance, and the reward awaits the soul."

So on the day appointed the host was marching to the place, and at the hour of twelve the preacher opened the "Word from the Sacred Book"—Mark 14: 9—"That she hath done shall be spoken of for a memorial of her."

So I preached the work of the good old Christian and the glorious end of "such a life, of life of everlasting joy."

The effort was well taken, and closed with thirty accessions, and their conversion, to be saved on the tune "Of Faith in the Blessed Redeemer."

I left there to meet an appointment with Rev. Israel McGowan, at Spartanburg. On my arrival one of the white citizens of the town called on the Reverend,

57. The verse is actually Luke 5:26: "And they were all amazed, and they glorified God, and were filled with fear, saying, we have seen strange things to day."

58. A reference to the prophet Elijah's encounter with the prophets of Baal on Mt. Carmel in 1 Kings 18. God consumes Elijah's sacrifice with fire as a sign of acceptance and answered prayer.

and invited him to hold his service in the Court House, that the white citizens could attend, "Our Church" being small, and promised to have all order and accommodation, and the Reverend accepted the kind invitation. And the Court House bell was rung, notifying the citizens of the hour of service, because of the parade of the common whites all day dressed in blood red shirts, and carrying Winchesters, preparing for the great Democratic campaign meeting on the next day.[59]

But resting on the promise of "Him whose words are sure and steadfast," "Fear not, I am with thee,"[60] I went up to meet a packed house. Seats were at a premium.

So I spoke from Galatians 6: 17—"Let no man trouble me, for I bear in my body the marks of the Lord Jesus."

The order of the press was remarkably grand. The vast crowd moved out as silently as "under a funeral dirge." The pastor and myself were the last to leave the house, and when we reached the street we hardly met a person, notwithstanding it was a pleasant moonlight night. I think the presence of the red shirts made the quickest at home, were the best place for the race.

My leaving the town on the next day several of the citizens came to the depot and assured me they would be pleased to have me come again. Their kind expressions brought to my mind the fact that "God has and is using all of my members as instruments in His hands to the glory of His Name."

I truly trust, young reader, as you not [*sic*] the life work of the writer, that you will conclude that you ought to present your members also as "instruments of righteousness unto God," to be used as He sees best to the glory of His Name.[61]

---

59 While the date of this event is unclear, the existence of the Red Shirts as a paramilitary group designed to instill fear in those who did not support the Democratic Party is well documented, particularly the group's determination to take back control of local and state offices from black and white Republicans in 1876 in parts of North and South Carolina. Various groups of mounted Democrats wearing red shirts rode through the streets of South Carolina communities to intimidate black voters before the November election, despite the presence of federal troops in some areas. On voting day, November 7, hundreds of black voters were turned away from the polls. For an interesting list of "Instructions to Red Shirts in South Carolina, 1876," see Paul D. Escott et al., eds., *Major Problems in the History of the American South*, vol. 2, *The New South*, 2nd ed. (Boston: Houghton Mifflin, 1999), 37–38. See also Powers, *Black Charlestonians*, 262–63.

60. The phrase is used in scripture over 150 times.

61. A reference to Romans 6:13: "Neither yield ye your members as instruments of unrighteousness unto sin: but yield yourselves unto God, as those that are alive from the dead, and your members as instruments of righteousness unto God."

I am en route for Rev. D. H. Allen's work at Greenwood, "this true and tried servant of God" met me on arriving at the depot, and conveyed me to the very pleasant home of Mrs. Maria Logan, the sainted sister to the twin, and noted Rev. Jefferson. Her house is noted as the "preachers' boarding place." This made my visit a little Paradisacal. I was asked by my sainted sister to help her pray that my coming to dispense the "word of truth to dying men" that some word may reach the heart of her husband, that may bring him to own the Lord.

At the age of 65 years, so we pledged to try the Lord on the old man's case. He would never be persuaded to attend the church, which was only one-fourth of a mile from his house, so I had to form a plan to get near to him, for he kept shy of all the preachers.

I called on him on the farm, to view his crop, and while walking around with him I told him I shall preach on Sunday morning, and asked him "to take me to church." He did not consent to this, but said he would hear me on Sunday. Then I told him when he came in to supper I should like to get his plan of planting so I could learn the boys at home. And after supper the Reverend had prayer before we left the room. So we caught him into prayers in honor to the Lady Preacher.

Sunday morning he begged me not to wait for him, or I shall be late, but that he will be there in time. Yes, he came, but sat out upon the steps of the church, but he said "he heard enough of my sermon," from Hebrews x: 3—"It is a fearful thing to fall into the hands of the living God."[62]

I was able to spend a part of the week at the request of the wife and daughter of the old man, who seemed as he seemed to have been since Sunday under a serious conviction, but he kept away from all in the house. His meals had to be sent to him on the farm. I was obliged to leave this good sister Logan on this day, so I sent his little son, now a man of family and a preacher of some merit in the M. E. Annual Conference, S. C., to tell him I was going, and wanted to say good-bye. So he came in with a sad look. Well, father, I am going, said I and we may never meet again in this world, but we must all meet at the "judgment seat of God." When we meet, on which "hand of God" shall I find you?

At this point in waiting for an answer, the heart grew faint, and the fountain of care and trust overflowed, and the tears of grief and repentance ran down his cheeks, and he handed me his right hand, saying: "Take me on the Lord's side, and I shall meet you there in that morning.' We called the Rev. Allen in, and though our time was limited for the train. His wife sent for the children

62. Hebrews 10:31.

to come up to the house, "and he was taken in to the church" as the ark of safety, and he came in just in time to escape the destroying flood.

"Saved just in time," for in less than four months later "the dear old man was called to leave time for eternity."

We had two miles to drive to meet the train, with twelve minutes to make it in. Yes, we just got there to get aboard the train, and not to get a ticket. But what of that? We took a man "who was in the hands of eternal death" to the Great Physician of the Soul, and left him in the arms of Eternal Life. "Hallelujah, he is saved."

I leave to meet an appointment with the Rev. Robert Andrews, of Sumter, S. C., brother to the all-round Christian gentleman and successful merchant of Sumter, William Andrews, and the second of no superintendent at any place, where he has stood as the "beacon light of Pisgah Church."

The Presiding Elder of the work, Dr. William M. Thomas, now of Columbia, met me and carried me to the pastor's residence, where we met the great revivalist and pastor of the Bethel A. M. E. Church at Columbia, the Rev. George Davis, who accepted my company in the services of the meeting. The writer was appointed to preach at eleven on the same day of arrival, and the merchants (white) closed their business for one hour, to come and hear the "Woman Preacher," who took John x: 14—"The Lord is my Shepherd, in trust that the name of God may be glorified."[63]

I preached for the Rev. David Harris, the sainted man of "God's Church." His work was at the upper end of Edgefield, styled as the Dark Corner. When the poor (untutored whites) take all advantage against the freedman, but this clean, meek, sainted man was highly regarded by the higher class of whites, and was defended on all sides by them.

On Monday, at 3 P. M., the white members, forty in number of the M. E. Church, came to hear the writer preach, and after service a Mr. Leneir, of Augusta, came with others to speak with me, and he bid me "God speed," and said you must be the "woman called to preach," for I could hardly keep my wife from shouting out, "Hallelujah, God's power is seen in the flesh."

I collected a nice little sum from the white friends for our little Williams' Mission at Orangeburg, S. C.

I leave here for my work at school. Well, you ask how can you stay away so long? That is all right. I think I told you before that I had the best disciplined school in the District, and the most obedient set of pupils. The rules of the

---

63. Appears to refer to the title of her sermon rather than to the quotation from scripture: "I am the good shepherd, and know my sheep, and am known of mine" (John 10:14).

school were carefully carried out by all, you shall hear no one murmuring about my acts.

The Reverend and thriving young preacher, H. W. Keith, of the N. E. Conference, when a boy 12 or 13 summers lived 6 miles from this school, and would walk those 6 miles every day and return, leaving a school within 2 miles of his home, and his parents objected to the labor of walking, and the duties at home, but he said like this to them: "I am willing to do all you want done, but let me go to a school that has style in it."

You see at once the forward and ascending mind of the boy, to "mount high," and whatever is his standard to-day in the race of life, he has, by his determined and persevering will, made for himself, reared upon a good alphabetical foundation.

I should not wonder at such a man succeeding in the pursuits of life, and I am alive "to see the full result" for some. You must see in your own perusal of this little book that the many calls in the missionary work have made these twelve years teaching very laborious for the ("poor weak nerves"), and having a former pupil of my school just returned from the State College at Columbia, S. C., prepared for service, you may remember the year in the change of the administration, when the "Confederates took the reins of power," the negro students were all turned out, and the College resumed "its old primeval," and Mr. John Williams is at his old home again.

I deemed it the best thing for me to do is to resign the school in his favor, as Principal of the same, but my resignation was not accepted, so I called on the officers and related the impossibility of my holding out with the double work.

And they then consented to his Principalship. Shall I stay in the school as assistant? He being a very genteel young man for sure, I accepted. As the great responsibility was off my shoulders, I was free to go, for my daughter could substitute me at any time to his assistance with the consent of the Trustees.

I was impressed that the work of the saving of souls was more valuable, for many of us could teach by the letters, but few of us can or do teach "by the precept of the Spirit."

"Praise God" for the mystery in the life of the Christian.

Hear this expression of a "child of God: "I am crucified with Christ. I die daily."[64]

---

64. A reference to both Galatians 2:20, "I am crucified with Christ: nevertheless I live; yet not I, but Christ liveth in me: and the life which I now live in the flesh I live by the faith of the son of God, who loved me, and gave himself for me," and 1 Corinthians 15:31, "I protest by your rejoicing which I have in Christ Jesus our Lord, I die daily."

He was so given over to Christ, that if he should meet death in the path of duty, though it should involve martyrdom, it should find him, like the Apostle Paul, in readiness.

This ought to be the knowledge of all "truly blest and sanctified of God." We ought to be ready for life, or for death, as Providence may decree.

Now, having more time for church work, the Rev. Lewis Prioleau,[65] now the pastor of Bethel A. M. E. Church, I being an old friend of his wife and self, solicited me to assist him as much as I could in the church, and in the absence of himself from his family of grown children, who were not the present wife's, which was quite a help to her.

Very naturally when the children arrived in their teens, and anxious to run over, they are not inclined to be controlled. I am proud, however, to tell you, dear reader, I found all in the system of love. I should have but very little trouble in controlling the three young ladies and one young gentleman, having also granted me a power for good over the young. The children of Rev. Prioleau were of high association, but somewhat preposterous. But remember this is the nature of all who are "in Egypt darkness of the soul," and there is no other remedy to be found but that of "the grace of God," begotten in His words, that can break down and destroy the strong and stubborn will of man, and "this opportunity of God" was nearer than it was ours to know.

In July of the present year is the month the farmers lay by working any more in the matured crops, and was considered as a little vacation from the field, and the church embraces this season of time to supply itself with spiritual food "to fertilize the soul" for the past drought and the coming frost. So they had a three days camping in the wilderness, about six miles from the town. I was asked to stay till the closing, on Monday, noon. There were some fine sermons preached by the visiting clergymen during the time of camping, and "the hungering and thirsting souls" were fed and feasted on the "words of God."

On Monday morning the Rev. Prioleau, "the sanctified man of God," came to me in the tent comfortless, saying: "My sister, I am sadly disappointed, we must close this meeting, and not one convert to crown our labors."

"Well," I said, don't despond, my brother, for I had a signal of His presence at the break of day, and He may yet come. Let us look for Him."

65. The father of Rev. George Washington Prioleau (see note 71).

I did not attend the early service, not feeling able to take the early dew, but got near its close at the love feast,[66] and in time to "testify of my faith in the love of God and His unfailing promises to save us in all, and under all circumstances."

Then came the exercise to break bread together, but moved by the inspiration of the Spirit, I moved out from my company and went into a group of sinners. The first to approach was the son of the Rev. Prioleau, demonstrating "the anxiety of my soul," for the unsaved "whom we are sent to bring to Christ."

Now, reader, you are one accusing me as being superstitious in my way of expressing things, but let me tell you, and you listen to me again, who of the children of man "shall know the words and works of the Lord?" Shall receive "honor of his Father, God, in heaven?"

Your mind on my extreme theology is still the same? Well, I don't like retraction, but I shall acknowledge to you as we are not living in the same atmosphere, very possibly cannot accept the language of the soul living above this mundane shore. Let us go on, and you may get higher towards the Spirit's power.

Well, I go on to the bread breaking with sinners. Here, my son George, eat this bread with me as a token that I love you, and as I "laid my hand upon his head," his heart grew weak, and the dear boy burst into tears. I was so overjoyed at this break down, my strength also failed. I hastened to bring his father to witness "the hand of God" as He moves among His people.

As I got up to the stand the Rev. Grant was told by Rev. Prioleau to give out the Doxology. I signaled him not to, and the Reverend begged him to obey the signal. Sung an inspiring hymn, and called four mourners, and six young persons came to the chancel for prayer, and the first of the group that found the Lord precious to his soul and shouted "Glory to God," was young Prioleau, and the second was his sister, now Mrs. E. Caldwell, of Charlotte, N. C. Miss Clarkson, now Mrs. L. Esemond Cleckley, of Orangeburg, S. C., and Mr. Roberson—"four souls saved in Christ." Thus the promised sign was verified with His presence, to bless and save.

At the end of the meeting" [*sic*] "Hallelujah. Praise the Lord."

Here I am made strong in my way of "knowing the Lord." Do you believe that "God makes himself familiar with His saints?" Well, let me tell you, now and forever. It is so determined in my mind. All the world of doubters, with other powers combined, cannot change or rescind it out from me. Now, the

66. A reference to the Communion service described in 1 Corinthians 11:20–34.

young man Prioleau, held dear to me as his message "sent from God," and he has proved himself as called of God, for after some months with the help of his father, he arranged to attend the Claflin University at Orangeburg,[67] resolving to do much in his studies to befit himself "to laud the Name of Him" who saved him that he could tell unto all the world "what the Lord hath done for his soul." I am again on trial to prove the mysterious, the mysterious call or gift of the writer. Well, here comes an order or letter, a request through the church, from the distinguished lawyer and Col. of the Columbia United States Regulars, R. B. Elliotte,[68] to make a call for the men and organize a militia, and to the order of the great man, Acting Enrolling Officer, the name of one hundred and four men were enrolled, with the selection of good officers, who came up to the campus three times a week for drilling, the writer acting as the ambassador during these days for the Republican party, keeping them to their pledge for union. There were to be held a convention of the two parties, the Democrat and Republican, to set before the voters the true platform for each side, but the freed men must keep out. The militia deemed it as much their right as any other set of men to be present at the great campaign meeting, so I agreed that they should muster on the campus at five o'clock in the morning of the day, and I was up the best part of the night arranging banners for the campaign to begin at 7 o'clock for the grand march of twelve miles, with their banners floating to the breeze with mottoes "We fought for our liberty" and "The Negro has come to stay with you white men." They requested me to be present, so I took the eight o'clock train, and to my surprise the company were arrayed at the station, and as I came from the coach they greeted me with three cheers. I hurried into the bus and they marched behind and ordered the driver to take me up to the stand, and as we arrived our P. E., the lamented Bishop R. H. Cain, selected

---

67. Claflin University in Orangeburg, South Carolina, founded in 1869, is the oldest historically black college or university in the state of South Carolina.

68. R. B. Elliotte was the Honorable Robert Brown Elliott (1842–84) and the first African American commanding general of the South Carolina National Guard. Born in Liverpool, England, he was a journalist and lawyer who practiced in Columbia. He was a member of the state constitutional convention in 1868, a member of the state's house of representatives (1868–70), assistant adjutant general of South Carolina 1869–71, a US congressman (1871–74), and returned to the state house as Speaker (1874–76). He had a successful candidacy for attorney general of South Carolina in 1876 but was forced out of office the following year when the last of the federal troops were withdrawn from South Carolina. Elliott moved to New Orleans in 1881 and practiced law until his death.

seats for the Rev. Mrs. E. Rodney Williams and the writer. We sat there to hear several speeches, but seeing them taking a turn for unpleasantness, we came down and entered a house nearby for safety from any row, but everything went on and out fairly good. Men raged in their speeches, but ended all right, so our company of men returned to their homes as safe as when they left them. They used their liberty to choose for themselves which is the right party for them to follow, and which is the wrong, as it was their liberty to execute it, but as the years go by what changes have we not seen, of trials and conflict, with the experience of victory and defeat in the warfare of right against wrong, the strong against the weak, the rich against the poor, intelligence against ignorance. Witth [*sic*] the knowledge of these noted facts before my mind's eye, constrained me to hard labor the best I could to obtain the knowledge of books, coupled with the "Gift of God," which no man living or dead could take away. And I have made myself over into bondage with the Book, as far as my poor health and poverty allowed, however these hindrances restrain me, yet my books and flowers keep me strongly in bondage. Deprive me of these and you have robbed me of my highest life. "As I am forgetting those things which are behind, I am reaching forth unto those things which are before,"[69] resolving to obtain those things which make life a power for good, a joy to self and a blessing to others. O, Praise the Lord for the great gift of the Holy Spirit, the third Person in the Godhead, viz: "God the Father, God the Son, God the Holy Ghost, the Triune God, the three personal Powers united into one great Being. Now, dear reader, this is as far as I dare go to take in, to understand the Theology of "Three Gods in One," "Glory and Praise to the Triune God, Hallelujah."

Wherever I go, wherever I be, whatever I do, I have before my mind the same united Powers working in their personal office in the interest of lost man.

I have just recovered somewhat from a serious attack of prostration and my physician advises me to move away to some place for rest or I shall not recover my usual little strength, and to my praise I had purchased a pretty little home as a resort for over pressed labors, so here comes the day. I also purchased a four acre lot in the business part of the town, and the gentleman from whom I purchased offered to build me a neat cottage house and wait on me for the

---

69. A reference to Philippians 3:13–14: "Brethren, I count not myself to have apprehended: but this one thing I do, forgetting those things which are behind, and reaching forth unto those things which are before, I press toward the mark for the prize of the high calling of God in Christ Jesus."

price of five hundred dollars, but I prized freedom so well that I wanted to feel sure I was my own Mrs. and was able to govern myself. I had already purchased a pretty little home in the negro village, settled by the lamented Bishop R. H. Cain, and named after the martyr President Abraham Lincoln, so I decided not to build here, but to dispose of the lot, and move down to the home already built, however kind people were to me I saw the need of leaving.[70] My experience in the past supported me in my move. I saw much that would hinder my peace of mind. It would be a thorn in the flesh of some big I to have another I of the same value in the eyes of the people, and I could better afford to vacate than one on whom they were depending in obedience to the Spirit. I am guided by it into all good works. I always felt that I could lose a little to save others from sinning. I have known men to fail in their business and laid their failure to the one be preceded. Especially shall that one live among the people to prove the accusation. On my return from a visit the Rev. Bowen, successor of the same church said to me as a compliment I suppose, "Well, teacher, I have never heard any one more talked of among the people than you, and no one has come to them yet is like their old teacher." This is just what I told you is the true cause of my leaving, and I am the more convinced that I did the right thing, or it would have been, "The old teacher won't let us do well, for fear we shall excel her in the art." O, my, but I am out, and far out at that, ninety-two miles away, but I am here to see about the land I sold to a young white man for three hundred dollars ($300). He paid on the bargain one hundred ($100), the balance to be paid in seventy-five days, with interest of fifteen dollars ($15.00), if not paid to date. So according to bargain he failed to meet it and I came to have full settlement. I called on him and produced the title in full for the land. So he paid me cash the two hundred dollars ($200) and the $15.00 in a check on Rogers & Pelzer, factors of Charleston, S. C. I left him the title to review and we would meet him at the Notary's office at nine in the morning. I went out of town about four miles to spend the night with an old friend. Now, reader, here comes in an eventful occurrence. After a pleasant evening, I went to rest in a pleasant little room and slept soundly, and in a vision I was notified that that the check I had would cost me some trouble to have it cashed, and instructed to

70. Lincolnville, South Carolina, was founded in 1867 by Bishop Richard Cain and six other men. It was incorporated in 1889 and is the last remaining black-incorporated town in the state. For further information on the community, see Hampton and Washington, *History of Lincolnville*.

return it back to the man, and not to sign the title until he shall cash it, or I may never get the interest paid me. Now here comes the question: how am I to get the title into my possession again? I awoke and called to my friends, Mr. and Mrs. Allen Miles, and related the vision unto them and requested that he should take me back to the town at seven o'clock to be able to execute the plan of my mind. For sure my friends had me to breakfast at half-past five and at seven I was in the gentleman's store. I met the clerk and asked him had the Boss left the title there for me to sign. The young man found it upon his desk and gave it to me. When the master comes in ask him to come over to the Justice's office to sign title. So I went in time to explain it all to the Justice and solicited his protection, told him I shall give the check back to have him cash it here by some of the merchants. Here he comes in. "Good morning, pretty good. Have you signed the paper?" "No, sir, and I cannot until you have some of the merchants of this place to cash it for you, if you have not that amount in your store." He bluntly refused, so I gave the check to the Justice to keep until it can be cashed and held the title in my pocket. The Justice then advised him to have it cashed as I refused to take it. So he was forced to do so. He brought over the cash and gave the Justice, and I gave the Justice the papers and declared to my signature. He gave me the money and I left the office for the man to pay the costs, and I took the train for Charleston and deposited the same out of all harm's way. Now what can you say about this? How will you leave it out of the Mysterious Life and Calling? Well, let me sing you one stanza, "O, hinder me not, for I will serve the Lord, and I'll trust him until I die." Then I proceeded to move home for good, never to have cause to come back but for a visit to my friends. However I meant to move in secret, yet it got around. How do I know it? Well, here comes my mail. This one postmarked Orangeburg, S. C., after three days return to Claflin University. Well, well, let us read it.

Dear Mother: I suppose I am allowed to call you so. To my great regret and sadness, I was informed that you made up your mind to leave Lewisville. I am very sad to hear of this. What will we do for society when the few who make up society leave? I was in hopes of preaching my first sermon in your hearing, that you may, above all others, criticize or comment on it, but alas my hopes is blighted. So it is in this world of sorrow, when we are enjoying the blessings and teachings of kind friends, something happens to make our hearts feel sad. I know not what to think of such a sudden conclusion you have come to. "Why go away? Why leave us in solitude?" Why leave your best friends? Think, for thirteen long years you have been teaching and laboring. Boys and girls you have reared to manhood and womanhood during this time. They may not see the good you have done yet, but they will. Now before you enjoy this blessing thoroughly you go away perhaps never to come back again. I wish you well but my dearest hope is blighted. I am sorry that I cannot be at home that I may get a parting blessing. Many months since I have seen you. I am doing well in school. I am taking the lead of my class and you may say one of the head of the school. I have finished two books Latin and one in Greek, and doing well in Theology. Pray for me that I may ever cling to the Rock. Tell me when you are going to leave that I may meet you at the train to receive a parting blessing and a kiss to remember you.

  I am, yours truly,

Son in Christ,

GEORGE W. PRIOLEAU.[71]

This is in part my dear boy's letter I had in reserve nineteen years up to this date as my heart's delight souvenir. Yes, his joy came to him again, for I did hear his maiden sermon in a mysterious way. He came home sick from school, and I was sent for to come and visit the circuit by the Rev. Hazel, pastor in charge. On my arrival I found my son at home, so I had to pay my morning visit and preach at the church seven miles away. And I arranged with him. Shall we be late returning? I shall ask him to act for me so it was understood, and as we came rather late to have an early sermon and they were all there in time he assumed my place. We got in time for his beginning, but I would not have him stop. So his heart was glad and so was his mother in Christ, and he made a good beginning in the warfare against the world, the flesh and Satan. He valiantly used the weapon of destruction to sin[g] "Glory to God in the highest."

71. George Washington Prioleau (1856–1927) was born a slave in Charleston, South Carolina, but rose to prominence as an AME pastor and professor of theology at both Wilberforce University and Payne Theological Seminary in Wilberforce, Ohio. Additionally, he served as one of only five Buffalo Soldier chaplains in the US Army. His wife, Ethel, also served closely with him. His experiences with extreme racism and discrimination led him to work with the NAACP. For more on G. W. Prioleau, see Frank N. Schubert, *Voices of the Buffalo Soldier: Records, Reports, and Recollections of Military Life and Service in the West* (Albuquerque: University of New Mexico Press, 2009), 214–16, 219. See also Brian G. Shellum, *Black Officer in a Buffalo Soldier Regiment* (Lincoln: University of Nebraska Press, 2010), 186–87; and Robert V. Morris and Julius W. Becton, *Black Faces of War: A Legacy of Honor from the American Revolution to Today* (Minneapolis: Zenith Press, 2011), 35.

In relating the incidents will prove to you the many trying cases I have had to undergo in my life's work. On a visit of our lamented Bishop Brown to the work, he with the pastor, Rev. Felix W. Torence went down to the lower church, St. Peter's, and I was engaged arranging his chamber to have him comfortable on his return. My daughter Anna was reading in the sitting room. Here comes a rap at the door. "Come," she said. Rap again. "Come," she said, I feeling not the least fear of any offense from anyone in the surrounding town, for white and colored citizens were my admirers and friends. So I very sternly called out, "Why not come in?" Advancing to the door, when it opened and I was fearfully shocked to have a white man enter in, but I gathered up my nerves and handed him a seat with all the grace of a Christian. I wanted him seated as he was so tall above me upon his feet, with his broad slouch hat on his head and a large Turkish pipe in his mouth. I saw at once this meant "Protect thyself." After getting him seated I goes into my bedroom and put my seven times revolver, cocked and ready for use, into my pocket and gave my noted signal for alarm. The neighbor, understanding it, sent a courier in to the marshal, so I got ready for battle. "Well, sir, what is your errand at my house? As we are under the protection of the marshal of the town and are told by him not to admit any strangers into our home, but you got in before we knew. You are a stranger to the town." "Well, ladies," he said, "my motive is good. I learned in the town that the teachers of the school's name were Simonds, and knowing that my brother has a colored family in Charleston, I came to see. Are you his daughters, that I may pay some attention to you." "Well, no, we tell you all in a word: our father is a colored man and that is all there is to it. And to still our minds, he said, "Now, ladies, my name is Simonds, and I am a gentleman and you need have no fear." "Sir," I said, "you ought to have proven that as you entered the door. I am not alarmed but for your rude act. Seated in my house with hat on and pipe in mouth. The most common man around here would not do it." "Oh," said he, "have me excused," then doffed his hat at his side and pipe put into hat. Here comes another rap. "Come," I said, and a colored man enters, one Canty of the place. "Well," says he to the man, "is these the ladies you are looking for? If not you had better go at once," and so he did, and as they got out of the gate I heard the voice of the marshal and many more shouting "Halt!" then "Let us go and hear what has been done to our teachers. Well, they were told that he was civil enough but they must have him to know the danger of coming to this house. They took him down to the village and had a rigid examination of his intentions of coming up to the schoolhouse. He made to them the same statement as he gave us, and declared had he any intention of evil he was unable to do any harm for that he was so uncomfortable in himself with lady standing before me. I found myself as weak as though I were sick, and would have left the house sooner but found it difficult to get up until that man came in and "she moved away from before me." I was known after he left that he was at large as a murderer of his own wife, and but the negro guard surely alarmed him for good that night, as he was never seen or heard of since. So we went to bed after committing myself and all that was mine into the hands of our Heavenly Father, and slept in peace, as He has promised to keep me under His care. The rumor ran high the next day over the town that our teacher silenced the revolver of the bushwhacker. "This slang given to such men of his character," and the power attached to the mysterious personage were our teacher were overshadowed by "the Holy Ghost" as a garment. What have you to say in the matter of this case? Have you cleared away the mist from the eye of faith enough to comprehend "God's mysterious power" as "He displays it through the instrument in His hand?" Have you heard the answer Jesus made to Nathaniel at his surprise that Jesus, a stranger, should call him by name? Jesus answered him, "I saw thee when thou was under the fig tree, and if you believe this thou shalt see greater things than these,"—Job 1: 47, 50.[72] What higher or greater do us finite creatures see than God's powerful workings among His chosen to "the honor and glory of His name," and you and I shall never see the time when the promises and "the power of Jehovah" shall fail us. *No, no*, a thousand time *no*; not one jot of it shall pass away unperformed, only when there shall be no God," no heaven, no angels, no earth, no man, no sin, no sickness, no sorrow, no devil, no death, no resurrection, no judgment, no hell.[73] Until these be true, "God's Words stand as His mediatorial throne on high," and shall be when rolling years shall cease to move or be no more. Since I believe this to be the only Trust, I deem it my liberty to look for greater things in "God's own way" than I have heretofore seen and accomplished in His name, as I am passing onward and upward through the degree of the Spirit, until I

---

72. The actual biblical citation is John 1:47, 50: "Jesus saw Nathanael coming to him, and saith of him, Behold an Israelite indeed, in whom is no guile!" and "Jesus answered and said unto him, Because I said unto thee, I saw thee under the fig tree, believest thou? Thou shalt see greater things than these."

73. A reference to Matthew 5:18, where Jesus says, "For verily I say unto you, Till heaven and earth pass, one jot or one tittle shall in no wise pass from the law, till all be fulfilled." The rhythm of the litany is reminiscent of Romans 8:35: "Who shall separate us from the love of Christ? Shall tribulation, or distress, or persecution, or famine, or nakedness, or peril, or sword?"

"can read my title clear to mansions in the sky" and I can bid farewell to every fear, when "eyes shall shed no bitter tears," when I shall reach that happy shore and be forever blest," where not a wave of trouble "shall roll across my peaceful breast," then I shall sing "Hallelujah, hallelujah, praise ye the Lord."[74]

Do you wonder where I am now out of this "transport of joys and triumphant glorious state?" Well, I am still rejoicing in the victory over inner sins as well as outer, and up now, in the mountain city, Greenville, S. C., called here by the lamented Rev. Samuel Gibbes, pastor of the Presbyterian Church, where I spend a week series of meetings, "the Lord was gracious toward us," and we had much to rejoice for. I have returned to meet my conference at Columbia, S. C. Bishop Brown, after four years, is again our presiding officer. We met under "God's promises," and had His presence, and success was ours. I returned home quite comfortable in mind that I am surely "God's chosen child," and have much cause to rejoice in the fact that we are not left comfortless nor alone, as we find so much of this element in the association of our Christian friends, in joy and comfort in so many different ways. Oh, how blest are we in everything that God moves our hearts to do, "Praise the Lord for the great salvation that saves to the uttermost in its blessing and redeeming power."[75]

I am home again on the sick list, prostrated. My physician says, "you shall be obliged to be quiet now." "Yes, sir. I believe you, as I am too prostrated to sit up, but don't banter me, as I am not dead yet." My belief was that Satan had me under trial and wanted me out of the field, as he had been whispering in my

74. The words come from stanzas 1 and 4 of Isaac Watts's (1674–1748) hymn "When I Can Read My Title Clear" (1707): "When I can read my title clear / to mansions in the skies, / I bid farewell to every fear, / and wipe my weeping eyes. And wipe my weeping eyes, / and wipe my weeping eyes, / I bid farewell to every fear, / and wipe my weeping eyes. // There shall I bathe my weary soul / in seas of heav'nly rest, / And not a wave of trouble roll, / across my peaceful breast. / Across my peaceful breast, / across my peaceful breast, / And not a wave of trouble roll, / across my peaceful breast." Interestingly, there is here another connection to Voltaire in the hymn's lyrics. One scholar has linked the hymn's title to the poem "Truth," composed by the British poet William Cowper (1731–1800). He compares the lot of Voltaire to that of a poor and believing cottager who "Just knows, and knows no more, her Bible true—/ A truth the brilliant Frenchman never knew: / And in that charter reads, with sparkling eyes, / Her title to a treasure in the skies."

75. This may be a reference to Hebrews 7:25: "Wherefore he is able also to save them to the uttermost that come unto God by him, seeing he ever liveth to make intercession for them."

own ear. Even with the Doctor and others, up to this day that these attack [*sic*] has unfit me for further use, but I have never believed it and never will until this building of mine has so decayed that it becomes to my safety to move out to a higher home.[76] So I saw blest to call the Lord and tell Him all about it, and that he must take care of these attacks and attend it Himself and in His own way. Praise the Lord, He has and been caressing and carrying me right straight through. We ought all understand that no one of us gets free from physical conditions any more than from sin. Have you ever noticed, dear reader, how Satan unwillingly gives testimony to the past state of experience, and torments us just where we are? And not where we were last year? See how wise the devil is. He looks and attends to the present time while some of God's people are standing on the past blessings. There comes an attack of Satan right on the spot he finds me at work. He means to be obeyed. He says, "Stop!" Here it is. Our P. E., Rev. Santiana Flagler, the great preacher and evangelist, sent me down to one of the missions to preach for him while he shall go to the lower church. When I got at the station I was met by one brother Thomas, who took me in charge to convey to the church a mile away, and he had but an ox cart for his wife's use, so I had to fair with her. We went all right and had a very commendable congregation. "The good Lord was with us," and I have sufficient to believe that God blessed His word to the saving of souls. And while I, with others, was rejoicing in sinners being saved, Satan was busy plotting my downfall. In getting into the cart to meet the train on its return, in waiting for the seat, the brother left the ox to light his pipe. The creature walked off, thinking all was right and I fell out and was carried back to my home with a broken hand. And from the wrong treatment of the physician in treating it as a sprain instead of a break, I almost lost the whole arm from inflammation that had set in the cap of the shoulder, and were I not carried to the city of Charleston and put under the skillful treatment of the famous Dr. W. L. Crum,[77] after some thirty days' suffering, my chance would have been very poor to save the arm. My daughter Anna had the Doctor to come up to my home to attend me, but he found it would not do. After paying me three visits up here, he said it was a necessity for him to see me every day as my arm must be saved. So he very kindly saw for a

76. A reference to 2 Corinthians 5:1: "For we know that if our earthly house of this tabernacle were dissolved, we have a building of God, an house not made with hands, eternal in the heavens."

77. William Demos Crum (1859–1912) was a noted African American physician who was born in Charleston and educated at the Avery Normal Institute, the University of South

pleasant place for me, and said come at once, but I was unable to be moved on that day, and I could not see my way to leave my home with money to go. I must rent a furnished room, but I must go or die. What shall I do? My daughter said to me as a comfort, "Did I not hear you say that the Lord is your provider?" How now, has he left you when you most need him?" Then I awaked out of my drowsy state and went right up to the Lord and said "Lord, I come to Thee for help." So I had the answer to go, and He will provide my needs. Here it comes at ten o'clock the next day. On the arrival of the train from the city two strange ladies call on me with the intent of purchasing a lot of land to build a house for the Home and being in want of money I agree to let them have it for twenty-five dollars, and they bind the bargain with twelve and one-half dollars, and the balance to be paid as soon as I can give them the titles for it, and here comes Elder Flegler[78] and Dr. B. F. Porter[79] to make arrangements to take me to the city as the Doctor requested, he bearing the expenses of the trip of daughter and self from home to the stopping place. But the mystery in the case. I was being led by both from the train to the trolley when I stepped upon a roll. I

Carolina, and Howard University. He began practicing medicine in 1881 and rose to national attention in 1902, when President Theodore Roosevelt nominated him, at the suggestion of Booker T. Washington, for the position of Collector of the Port of South Carolina. The nomination drew fierce criticism from Southern Democrats. According to the *New York Times* (March 6, 1903), "the Committee on Commerce found nothing in Crum's record to object to. He was shown to have the ability, the character, and the popularity, even with the whites, to recommend him for the place. His color was the objection." Despite the opposition, Roosevelt held his position and Crum was appointed. A more bitter battle ensued over his renomination in 1909, resulting in Crum's resignation. See Booker T. Washington to Theodore Roosevelt, March 1, 1903, Theodore Roosevelt Papers, Manuscript Division, Library of Congress, Washington DC, available online at the Digital Library, Theodore Roosevelt Center at Dickinson State University, Dickinson, ND, http://www.theodorerooseveltcenter.org/Research /Digital-Library/Record.aspx?libID=040544&f=%2fSearch.aspx%3ff%3dDigitalLibrary %26searchTerms%3dBooker%2520T.%2520Washington.

78. Appears to be the same Rev. Santiana Flagler as above.

79. Dr. B. F. Porter was the pastor of the Morris Brown AME Church in Charleston and a practicing physician. Along with Bishop Richard H. Cain, he was intricately involved in the Liberian emigration movement of 1878. The violent political campaign of 1876, along with the earlier work of the American Colonization Society, made emigration to Liberia an attractive option for many African Americans. On July 26, 1878, Morris Brown AME Church hosted a mass meeting of over 4,000 black people to celebrate the thirtieth anniversary of the Liberian Declaration of Independence. At that meeting, Dr. Porter proposed the formation

stooped down and picked it up and put it in my cloak pocket, not knowing what
it was, until I was at rest, then told Anna to see what was that I picked up on my
way and lo, she found the contents to be about nineteen dollars! I heard no
advertisement of a loss, so it was my helper in sickness. Then I held my membership in Society of the Ladies of Ruth, so this Society paid my sick dues weekly,
one dollar and twenty-five cents. So with these showers of blessings coming in
to me, daughter was able to get me all needed comforts. Could I help singing,
"Praise God from whom all blessings flow?" I praise Him forever.

The pastors of the churches were very kind to me in my distress. Rev. R. H.
Nichols administered to my wants in a financial way that is a blessing to be
returned. The Rev. Norman B. Sterritt and Elder P. S. Jefferson remembered
me. I had a visit from one of the old mothers in Israel, Sister Middleton, who in
her way tried to comfort me for I was having from the agony of my hand convul-
sions at intervals, so I was ill. On the old Christian leaving me, she said, "Don't
you be discouraged, my child. Satan only means to discourage you under this
blow, but cheer up. You shall be able to go out upon the field of the Gospel and
do great battle for the Lord against the adversary." So we rejoiced together in
hope of a glorious victory. By and by I was unable to help myself in dressing,
for one year under sore affliction. "I could not call it sweet, but I found it good
to bear, as it brought me closer to Jesus, and in bowing at His feet, and I received
abundant mercy there." *Hear, hear, listen!* Rejoice not, my enemy, for though I

---

of the Liberian Exodus Joint Stock Steamship Company with 30,000 shares of stock at $10
per share. Porter would serve as the company's president. Bishop Cain ran a standing editorial
in his *Missionary Record* titled, "Ho for Africa! One million men wanted for Africa." Prominent
African Americans were part of the cause, including H. N. Bouey and Martin Delaney, along
with other ministers with whom Riley worked, like Flagler. Black churches at first opposed
the movement but later incorporated its message as part of their evangelical mission to carry
the gospel to Africa. The *Azor*, a ship commissioned to support the movement, set sail in May
with 206 emigrants. Several misjudgments undermined the success of the voyage. Twenty-
three passengers died from fever before reaching Africa. The food and water supply were
insufficient, there was no licensed physician on board (Porter did not travel on the maiden
voyage), and there was reported logistical mismanagement. While ultimately some emigrants
to Liberia achieved success, many considered the *Azor* voyage a general failure. See George
Brown Tindall, *South Carolina Negroes, 1877–1900* (Columbia: University of South Carolina
Press, 2003), 153–68. For a discussion of the role of black physicians during Reconstruction,
see Marion Brunson Lucas, *A History of Blacks in Kentucky: From Slavery to Segregation, 1760–1891*
(Louisville: Kentucky Historical Society, 2003).

was down, I rise again. Where are you now, you ask? Well, I am out in battle array for victory. I am called by Elder Hiram Young of Columbia Conference to go with him to Aiken church at his quarterly meeting, Rev. Simon Beared, pastor, where he wanted me to preach one of the three sermons for the day with the Rev. Carolina, Father to the Sankey and Moody of our church, as in the power of the Spirit, using to his advantage and singing to profit. The gifted man, Rev. W. P. Carolina, brother to the loving wife of the efficient and esteemed secretary of the S. C. Annual Conference, and the St. John of the pulpit, as he expounded the love of his Master in that gentle, earnest, believing, persuasive manner, so much like the Savior's loving John, claiming his hearers to the acceptance of God's words. Praise the Lord, for Rev. C. W. McQueen,[80] the Elder, closed his conference at Aiken with many confessing the name of their Lord. I was requested to stay over as help to the Rev. Brother Beaird [*sic*]. You remember the writer's apology in the introduction of this little book. Well, hear it again, that some young man or woman while reading may by some statement or expression find out their calling or see the cause to prepare themselves to be used to the glory of their Maker, but it came to pass long before the little book was consented to be written. While preaching at Aiken, the lamented young clergy of the Episcopal persuasion was struck by the zeal of the writer and made a resolve to go to Jesus and have himself endowed for the glory of His name. He died with sword in hand, all stained with the blood of the enemy. Another little school boy and pet of the little school of infants heard a sermon from his teacher at Sumter, where they were living at the time. He had grown out of the infant school. He, however, declared himself on the Lord's side, to carry his name. Already he caught the Spirit that elevates the mind and adorns the man. This little William L. Bulkley is the son of the lamented Rev. Vincent H. Bulkley of the M. E. Church. Young Bulkley is now a man of great note, having mastered all the science necessary for any position chosen by him in the material or the spiritual world. Praise the Lord Jehovah. He is to-day "a polished shaft in the hand of God."[81] As a graduate of the Claflin University, he reflects

80. Rev. C. W. McQueen served as one of the pastors of the Bethel AME Church in Summerville, South Carolina. The church, located at 407 South Main Street, is still in existence. He also served as the pastor of the Morris Brown AME Church of Charleston, South Carolina, which is also still in existence and located at 13 Morris Street.

81. A reference to Isaiah 49:2: "And he hath made my mouth like a sharp sword; in the shadow of his hand hath he hid me, and made me a polished shaft; in his quiver hath he hid me."

back upon her town unimpeachable honors. One has said, "Like teacher, like pupil." I am so glad that my little pet has imbibed the inner spirit of his old teacher, but he is now among the prophets, pointing the nations of the earth as he shall meet them into the way of salvation in the name of Jesus. He has chosen a wife of lovable family, and is truly crowned with a virtuous gem of womanly grace and beauty.[82]

Mail comes? Yes, let us have it. Well, my daughter, here is a letter from your sister Estella Matthews, inviting us to come and spend a season of rest with her in the city of New York. "Oh, I trust, my darling (this is her pet name for mother) that you will accept and let us go to see my only sister." We had not seen her since she was married, so I made all arrangements and let our moving stay until our return from North, and on the sixth of June we took shipping for New York. Our P. E. hearing of our leaving, the Rev. Cain wrote a letter of introduction to the pastor of the Bridge Street A. M. E. Church,[83] the Rev. Theodore Gould,[84] where Mrs. Matthews held her membership at the time. She went from New York to Brooklyn to attend her class every week, and Sabbath services as well, so we attended the service with her as we were of the same household of faith. We all attended the Wednesday evening service and during preaching the Rev. came down the aisle asking, "Is there a Mrs. Riley present?" to my astonishment. I was introduced to him by Mrs. Matthews, and he asked me to come up to the front with him, and took me into the chancel

82. A probable reference to William L. Bulkley, the sole black public school principal in New York City in 1909 and an original member of the National Committee for the Advancement of the Negro, which was later renamed the National Association for the Advancement of Colored People (NAACP). Riley's description of him as having once lived in South Carolina "at the time" with his family and her New York connections make the association probable.

83. According to the church's website (http://www.faithstreet.com/church/bridge-street-ame-church), "The Bridge Street African Wesleyan Methodist Episcopal Church is the oldest continuing black congregation in Brooklyn. This unique congregation, located in the heart of Bedford-Stuyvesant, was organized in 1766 and incorporated in 1818. It traces its missionary origins to Captain Thomas Webb, a British convert of John Wesley and the father of Methodism in America." The church is currently located at 277 Stuyvesant Avenue.

84. For an image of Rev. Gould, see New York Public Library Digital Collections, http://digitalgallery.nypl.org/nypldigital/dgkeysearchdetail.cfm?trg=1&strucID=212302& imageID=1245704&total=1&num=0&word=Gould%2C%20Theodore&s=3&notword=&d= &c=&f=2&k=0&lWord=&lField=&sScope=&sLevel=&sLabel=&imgs=20&pos=1&e=w.

and had me to close the service of the evening. I was asked to say something in closing. I accepted, just to make known my true position at home—just as a common school teacher among the poor, destitute children and solicited the aid in books for my Sabbath school. And my plea kindly granted with the aid of the Rev. S. W. Hazel,[85] then an officer of the church. The Rev. Gould collected and shipped to my home to meet me on my arrival without cost, a box of books donated by the members of the S. S. and the church. The Rev. asked that I should preach for his people before I return South, but I declined as not feeling able to do so.

Here comes the Rev. Henry Matthews,[86] the father-in-law of Mrs. Matthews, inviting me to visit his church at Patterson, N. J. I accepted to go. So on Saturday we met him at the train and away we went, arriving in full time of the day to walk around and see callers and rest well at night. I was expected to preach for him, but would not attempt to do what I was sensible to know I could not. On my attending evening service, I was pressed to the point and found I must do something in the way of talking so I trusted the Lord and made a little address. In it I chided them for not having their own house of worship, as we down South were worshiping in our own house. But shall the white man say to you to-morrow "Come out of my school house, where will you go?" Well, my little talk, however, has done much good, for they commenced that very night, in honor of the teacher from the South, to collect at that meeting for the purchase of a place of worship, and we collected then and there cash donations amounting to twenty-five dollars. Then I announced that shall they swell the amount to one hundred dollars by the time I reached home South, I shall send the trustees ten dollars of my wages, and to my astonishment in less than twenty days I received a letter from the Rev. Henry Matthews that they had cash in hand one hundred and twenty-five dollars, and in my return answer I expressed the ten dollars promised by me. I was informed in the next letter, some month previous, of the purchase of a lot with the building of a white congregation purchased and moved upon the lot, with the petition to return my visit and enjoy with them the result of my success in the service "of the ever to be remembered

85. Rev. S. W. Hazel is listed in the *Centennial Encyclopedia of the African Methodist Episcopal Church*, vol. 1, ed. Richard R. Wright and John Russell Hawkins (Philadelphia: Book Concern of the A.M.E. Church, 1916), 357.

86. Rev. Henry Matthews is listed in the *African Repository and Colonial Journal*, vol. 5, of the American Colonization Society (Washington, 1830).

night." These are the words of our Lord: "Fear not, I am thy shield. Fear not, for I have heard the cry of thy distress and blessed thy fainting soul."[87]

Oh, what? A letter from my dear spiritual son? Well, let us hear it. Well, surely he is a preacher in charge of a congregation.

> Powers Shop, Lawrence Co., S. C.
>
> DEAR MOTHER:—I am sorry to hear you are unwell. Hoping this may find you better. Wrote you a letter asking you to reply to the one I wrote before. On last Sunday I attended a big meeting, and there was a thousand people there, and I gave out my meeting, beginning on the 9th of Sept, and stated that you will be with me, now relying on you, that you will come. *Please* not say *No. Please* not let my word fail. Come, *please, mam,* come, and I will do all I can for you, and you need not do hard work when you come. Others beside my people will be happy and pay well just to see you with me in the pulpit. Come and help us. Do come and don't fail me. Now if you claim me as your son, come and prove it. *Come* and claim me, and in so doing you shall claim others. Do reply this week without delay.
>
> Your son in Christ,
>
> GEORGE W. PRIOLEAU.

Well, how could I stay away from such a solicitation as this? O, yes. My child would mistrust my interest in his success. I was quite poorly at the time of his letter, but I trusted the Lord to help me go to him, so answered, shall it please the Lord, I shall be with him, even could I not be able to labor. I believe he would rather have a sick mother than have no mother at all. Praise the Lord, I am with him and am able to attend the meeting. "And the Lord stayed with us and I was glad to be with the people, for much good work was done, for many were saved in Jesus' name on the terms of the Gospel." The most singular work of the meeting:—A young white man attending the meeting invited the preacher and his mother to come and dine with him. On arriving there I found him to be the father and husband of a colored family, and he claiming membership in the Presbyterian white church. I took the opportunity of expostulating with him in his spiritual state, that he was doing no good for his soul, nor his wife

87. Perhaps this is a reference to the biblical patriarch Abraham's early encounter with God in Genesis 15:1 as he was waiting for the fulfillment of the promise of an heir: "After these things the word of the Lord came unto Abram in a vision, saying, Fear not, Abram: I am thy shield, and thy exceeding great reward."

and children, as they can't follow him, but he can follow them with all grace, and he may become their leader and teacher, and look forward for a great reward for his work. He at once saw the state of things and consented to come where he could do good for himself and others. Now the time came for me to speak. We had a good number of whites, he in among them, and when the doors of the church were opened, the preacher said to me, "Your bird is roosting too high to get down," but in my entreaties and warnings of delay the young man arose and came out from among them "and gave me his hand" and joined in the church of his family. The members all knew his standing and received him with joy. He with the other choiced a leader. "O, what a victory over Satan and Sin," "Glory to the Lamb that was slain to redeem the sinful man."

On my leaving the work, my new member and white son brought me his photo and presented it to me as a reminder of him in prayer. How happy I am to have set this young man upon the road that leads to true righteousness. Let us always follow the example of the Lord Jesus, who went about doing good. For example, my dear reader, is said to be the very best teacher outside of the grand old school of experience. Yes, and how proud we ought to be for this class of men and women in among the race, because their experimental lives and examples in their work and character are transmitted, reminding us "that as they did, we may do, and make our lives sublime.

I am at home to rest. I did not attend the conference, as I was quite unable to do so from the same old thorn in the flesh, but we have a change in Bishops in the person of Right Rev. William Fisher Dickerson[88] and Rev. William M. Thomas, P. E., who brought me on his return to the first quarterly conference of Bethel A. M. E. C. Let me say of this Rev. what he is worthy of having, a veteran of the army of God. No greater can be said of him, nor less than that,—he is a clear cut Christian gentleman, a good man, a pattern for young men.

The paper he handed me was from the new Bishop. I must have been chosen by some of the servants of God for the work, as the paper read thus:

> Under protection of Almighty God, A. M. E. Church. Credentials. This is to certify that the Rev. C. S. Riley is appointed Mite Missionary agent, the said agency being under the jurisdiction of the Columbia Annual Conference of the

---

88. William Fisher Dickerson (1844–84) was born in Woodbury, New Jersey, and licensed to preach in 1867. He began his itinerant career in 1870 and was elected the thirteenth bishop of the AME Church in 1880. He also served as the chairman of the board of trustees of Allen University from 1880 to 1884.

A. M. E. Church. Given under my hand and the denomination seal, at the Episcopal rooms, this fourteenth day of December, 1882.

Your next conference will be held in Spartanburg, S. C. Signed in behalf of said conference,

WM. F. DICKERSON, Presiding Bishop.

This letter followed the credentials. I think I shall let you hear it in part. All shall help to bring out more clearly the title of the little book.

Columbia, S. C., 1-5-'81.[89]

DEAR SISTER RILEY:—I was glad to hear from you I meant to sit down and map out a campaign for the entire conference. I requested the pastors to have you assist their respective congregations on some week night to organize our Mite Missionary Society and explain the object of the same. Now you write to Sister Mary Campbell, 1923 Nor. 11 St., Philadelphia, and ask her to send you a supply of M. M. S. Constitutions.[90] It is my request to the pastors that they will take up a collection for you, and by that means I hope you may secure a living and traveling expenses while you pursue your errand of love. This is all the instruction I decide to give you at this time. Let me hear from you occasionally.

Yours fraternally,

WM. F. DICKERSON.

These unsolicited highly favored positions is in part why my friends and admirers constrained me to the work, giving the world of critics so much advantage over the writer. O, well, it does not hurt so much after all, for as a student in the school of Christ and teacher of the lower grade, He will not criticize us in presenting our report.

89. Based on the date of Dickerson's correspondence and Riley's own references, the date should be 1883.

90. The wife of Bishop Jabez Pitt Campbell served as the first president of the Women's Parent Mite Missionary Society (WPMMS), founded on May 8, 1874, the AME's first women's missionary organization. It held its first convention in Philadelphia on August 11. Between 1874 and 1878, Campbell created local societies and performed missionary work in Haiti, Santo Domingo, and West Africa, while focusing the domestic efforts of the organization in the North. She is also listed at this address as a contributor in the January 1900 edition of *The Peacemaker and Court of Arbitration*, edited by a Committee of the Universal Peace Union (UPU). The UPU, founded by Alfred Love (1830–1913) in 1866, was headquartered in Philadelphia and opposed war of any kind. The organization ceased operations with Love's death.

1883 found me comfortably housed at my little country home for good, until I am called to move away by the Giver of all Good, and I began at home first to organize the Mite Society, assisted by the round-the-world-Missionary, Mrs. J. K. Borney [*sic*],[91] of Providence, R. I., and was able by the vigilance of its members to send six dollars to the conference by the pastor, but when the minutes of the conference came to us, it was found that the report of six dollars was given to the other named church and nothing said about the Society of the church that sent the amount, so technical president was indignant and withdrew from the Society and we never could get the members together and the work went down. Our Conference number of preachers increased so rapidly which made it very burdensome to meet in a small town, and it became necessary to divide and name the upper part Columbia Conference and let the old name remain to the lower division. And I fell in the upper part as living in the upper and have not as yet been transferred. The brethren made no difference with what part of the body I held to. They were all kind in their treatment toward me and some of them said they were very proud of the only girl child in the ministerial family, and were proud at any time to have me in their pulpit and under their care. Well, I have been an acceptable member in their midst since 1871, laboring for the supply of the church and gaining of souls, with all credit to my calling, irrespective of standing or creed, and the secret in my holding up and out these many years is trusting in God to carry on His plans and leave the ranting to the formalist, and accept the teaching of St. Paul, twelfth chapter to the Romans: "Present your bodies a living sacrifice, holy and acceptable as your reasonable service,"[92] and to do this I have labored earnestly and believingly, and as strong as is my faith in the Word of God, keeping in mind it is better to

91. Mrs. J. K. Barney of Providence, Rhode Island, was influential in early prison work and was a part of the Christian Endeavor Society, formed in 1881 in Portland, Maine, to bring youth to accept Christ and work for him. Young people were shown that the church cared for them and were allowed to express themselves while participating in useful tasks. The organization sponsored publications, programs, and events for youth and was maintained through private donations that often came from the youth themselves. By the end of the nineteenth century, Christian Endeavor was in the headlines of many major American newspapers. Still in operation, the organization is considered the source of modern-day youth ministry. See Frances Williard, *Woman and Temperance: Or, The Work and Workers of the Women's Christian Temperance Union* (Hartford: James Betts & Co, 1888), 585.

92. Romans 12:1: "I beseech you therefore, brethren, by the mercies of God, that ye present your bodies a living sacrifice, holy, acceptable unto God, which is your reasonable service."

live long in the Gospel to the honor of God, as no one will thank you for killing yourself by ranting out the message of the Lord, and when you are dead, men will call you a fool. I have heard their murmurings, after receiving the message of such, saying they were unbenefitted, occupying the time over the loquacity of the messenger. I don't believe it is the way God's message is to be delivered. I believe that what I am is of more importance than what I do, and the providence of God makes me responsible for the careful preservation and proper use of the powers granted. I have no right to needlessly throw away the energy which God has granted me. As God's messengers, you and I, dear reader of this class, have a right, I believe it a duty as well, to guard against excess and avoid danger and to abstain from everything which can injure or destroy us. There is no one to care for me as I can for myself, so I have tried and always will to have food, raiment, rest, sleep, and protection so to befit myself for the best and most lasting service for the glory of God and the good of mankind. Praise the Lord, Amen.

I am writing this little book in my fifty-seventh year, with an unbroken zeal for the spread of the Gospel, with my lungs as sound as a girl's, and my voice losing very little in sound. Soundness of character and more faith in God is the all needful for success, so I go on in the same good old way.

Mail comes? Yes, give it here. There is a letter for the Rev. Elias J. Gregg.[93] Well, hear what he says to us from the hill country, Marion, S. C. In brief:

> Dear Mother, I shall look for you to be with me on coming Sabbath. Be sure to come. We shall look for you.

Yes, I must obey the children. When mother is wanted she must go. So I at once arranged to meet his call, and sure he met me with his fine grey horse and

93. Elias J. Gregg was the pastor of Wise Chapel AME in Marion, South Carolina. The church is still in existence and is located at 1748 Wise Chapel Court. He was a past general secretary of the Allen Christian Endeavor League in Charleston, South Carolina, and in 1889, he organized the building of Flegler High School in Marion, South Carolina, named for the aforementioned Rev. Santiana Flegler. The school served as a feeder for Allen University. He is also perhaps one of the founders of the Afro-American Industrial and Benefits Association, founded in 1901, Florida's first African American insurance company. The group of founders was connected with the AME Church. See Charles Spencer Smith, *A History of the African Methodist Episcopal Church: Being a Volume Supplemental to a History of the African*

buggy, and speeded me to his pleasant family without delay. O, here comes the dear little boys to meet me at the door. O, yes, a kiss for all. Then mamma comes in for hers. The children echo their excellent parents in true friendship and love. I always find myself in extreme happiness with this well ordered family, husband, wife and children. This is a beautiful Sabbath morning for a six mile drive to the little A. M. E. Wise Chapel where the congregation were eagerly waiting for the Word of Life. I strove in my usual manner to impress the words selected from Jer. 8: 22, "Are there no balm, etc."[94] Many believed on the Lord Jesus and expressed saving faith and believers were renewed in faith and hope and made afresh their covenant "for God to live and for him to die." In closing the service, the dignified pastor, Rev. Gregg, gave me a laudable introduction as his mother in Christ and the daughter of the S. C. Conference, when a dear old Christian lady arose and said, "No, pastor, she is not that, but she is the daughter of the Lord Jesus," and in the twinkling of an eye I saw deep down in niche of that humble but rich mind, this veteran of the cross carrying the idea that name "Daughter of the Conference" did not adorn sufficient for the benefit she received of the message delivered and the souls that were born of God. I was introduced to this dear lady as Sister McQueen and that she is the mother of Rev. C. W. McQueen, pastor of the Morris Brown A. M. E. Church, of Charleston, S. C. I wondered could he be less than proficient hailing from such a specimen of silent wisdom, but hark, what do I hear? She has gone up to claim her membership to the "church where congregation ne'er breaks up, where the service never ends." Glory to God on high. She is resting over yonder in the glory land from labor to reward. I met her in Charleston at the parsonage of Morris Brown church where she was spending the last of her years with her beloved son. I shall not soon forget her urgent appeal to me to return with her. Had I been able to grant her request, I should have been there. I should have seen her leaving us for the better land. However, I shall meet her again where parting is unknown.

Mail again? Yes, where from? Open it. Let me hear what the Lord shall do with his child. Letter from the Bishop, let us hear it.

Methodist Episcopal Church, by Daniel Alexander Payne, D. D., L.L.D., Late One of its Bishops, Chronicling The Principal Events in the Advance of the African Methodist Episcopal Church from 1856 to 1922 (Philadelphia: Book Concern of the AME Church, 1922), 367.

94. Jeremiah 8:22: "Is there no balm in Gilead; is there no physician there? Why then is not the health of the daughter of my people recovered?"

The Episcopal residence, Taylor St., Columbia, S. C. Rev. C. S. Riley:

Dear Sister, I had thought to transfer you to the old S. C. Conference, but he work I am deeply interested in needs a true Missionary, one whose whole heart is in the progress of the Gospel, and the brethren have selected you to be he one the most suited for the work. I desire that you may so arrange to go at nce, not that you shall do so great amount of work, but go and gather up the agment, and we may yet rejoice together over victory won. Go, my sister, and od go with you. Enclosed find your credentials. Well, well, this is God's. "How marvelous are His ways."

Pastoral Credential, A. M. E. Church. This is to certify that the Rev. C. S. Riley is appointed to the pastoral charge of Chester Mission, the said Mission being under the jurisdiction of the Columbia Annual Conference of the A. M. E. Church. Given under my hand and the denominational seal at the Episcopal room, this fourth day Feb., 1884. Signed in behalf of said conference,

WM. F. DICKERSON, Presiding Bishop.[95]

Now, dear reader, just to think. Notwithstanding this unsought for approbation from the hand of so great a leader of the church, higher still, the head of all the church, yet I must bear the cringing of the pigmy-minded to the acceptance of the honored title, but the Bishop wrote and sealed it, and the writer records it forever to stand in the face of the objectors who understand the sense of the Rev. title to one held in great respect as a deserving address to the true character the favored of the Lord. Being in the army 33 years, unapproachable, is no small gain for a woman fighting the battle single-handed and alone in weakness, affliction, poor, and oppressed, but with God on my side I go valiantly onward, fearing no defeat. No one knows what they can not do under the leadership of the Holy Spirit, whose office is to teach us in all our ways, and lead us into all victory, praise the Lord.

I have always sought the association of the wise and strong and so find myself in such without any particular effort on my part. It seems just to come to me so. Well, I did not tell you how long and how I served the Chester work. Well, I tell you now. I started to go, and got as far as Winnsboro to see the

95. Riley's appointment as the pastor of Chester Mission in Chester, South Carolina, in 1884 by Bishop Dickerson was virtually unheard of in the early AME Church. Unfortunately, because of a bad storm, Riley never worked with the church. Instead, the Bishop came to town and authorized her to assume the position of Conference Missionary.

treasurer of the Missionary funds to have him give me sufficient cash, but he had no money on hand, so I stayed over with the pastor, Dr. C. W. Crosby, arriving there on Friday, and on Saturday a severe storm passed over Chester and very much damage was done to the town. Everybody was on a run on Sunday. Many came into Winnsboro for safety, and as the Bishop is to be here the next Sabbath to serve the church I staid over to meet him so he took me back to Columbia with him, and told me to go and assume the position as the Conference Missionary and the brethren will receive me and give me aid as I might serve them. So you have my endorsement to visit the churches as a helper in spiritual work. You see, there is no "flag of truce in this war."

We must fight. It's "go on, go on." Till the battle is gained, until the enemies are all imprisoned forever in the dark domain.

I told you so. Here is an epistle from Rev. Thomas Evans, of the M. E. Church, calling me to assist in a pitched battle against the enemy to our cause. My arm being still in sling, I had to have my daughter Anna with me for help. "Anything my sister you may do, so you come." Well, we are here, at the very pleasant Brother Evans, and took charge of the Jervey Chapel, situated in a turpentine belt,[96] controlled by A. M. Price. The woman preacher drew these careless hands of the Pine every evening, and the service did much good during the week meetings. We called a testimonial meeting for Friday evening and news came to us that the young men of the Pine refused to eat all of Friday. One of the number refused to drink water, and said, "he had his full in the love of God." Yes, indeed, they were all at the meeting. Eighteen in number, with their work master accompanying them and seated on the front with the boys behind him, the master seemed out of the business, but when the young men began to tell what the Lord hath done for their souls with so great zeal, the master got aroused. From the flame of the Holy Spirit, he arose and cried out, "Fire, fire, in my soul. I am all afire," and the whole business caught afire, and

96. Also called a turpentine camp or naval store. The turpentine industry developed in America during the colonial period to support England's foreign trade. During the nineteenth century, the industry spread throughout the Carolinas and Georgia, supported mostly by slave labor. After the Civil War, blacks continued to work in the camps, often accompanied by their families and under conditions akin to those associated with sharecropping. For an interesting history of the industry, see Douglas A. Blackmon, *Slavery by Another Name: The Re-Enslavement of Black Americans from the Civil War to World War II* (New York: Anchor Books, 2008), 173–75, 339–41, 366–67.

Satan's camp burned to its destruction. Then we sang "Glory to God for His redeeming power, which save to the uttermost till we shall sin no more,"[97] and before I departed for my home I organized the converts into a society for their spiritual and material aid, and entitled it "The Jervey Watchman," after the pastor who erected the little mission church. They were to assemble themselves every Wednesday evening for prayer, or to give their experience of the past week, or their growth in grace. You see our work is not in vain in the Lord.

As soon as arrived at home, the first part of my mail was from a call to Columbia, S. C. My elder, Hiram Young, solicited me to assist the Rev. T. H. Jackson, pastor of the Bethel A. M. E. Church, in his revival. I served three nights, which resulted in four converts and eight accessions. I am truly proud to name the very remarkable wife of the excellent, successful business and Christian gentleman, Brother Palmer of Columbia, S. C., and father of the present young wife of the young Joseph. The not to be overcome Rev. W. D. Chappelle, D. D., secretary S. S. Union, Nashville, Tenn.[98] This is my pride, dear reader, to give honor where it is due in the example of the Master.

There comes the Elder, appointing me to go up to a place called Pudding Swamp, twenty miles above Maysville, to serve the church on Sunday and

97. Quoted from the fifth stanza of "And Are We Yet Alive," lyrics by Charles Wesley, 1749: Then let us make our boast, / Of His redeeming power, / Which saves us to the uttermost, / Till we can sin no more.

98. William David Chappelle (1857–1925) was born in Winnsboro, South Carolina, to Henry and Patsy (McCrory). Sources are unclear whether or not he was born enslaved. After being educated at a school funded by Northern Presbyterians, he was converted to the AME Church and graduated from Allen University. He served as the university's president from 1897 to 1899 and as the chairman of its board of trustees from 1916 to 1925. He served eight years as a pastor in the AME Church, ten years as a presiding elder, as the Secretary of the Sabbath School department of the AME Church, and was consecrated the thirty-seventh bishop of the AME Church in 1912. In 1918, he met with President Woodrow Wilson at the White House to "protest lynchings, mob violence, Jim Crow laws, and discrimination of all kinds directed at African Americans." See D. W. Culp, ed., *Twentieth Century Negro Literature, or, A Cyclopedia of Thought on the Vital Topics Relating to the American Negro by One Hundred of America's Greatest Negroes* (Atlanta: J. L. Nichols, 1902), 62; and Milton C. Sernett, *Bound for the Promised Land: African American Religion and the Great Migration* (Durham, NC: Duke University Press, 1997), 47.

hold the meeting over for the Bishop and himself on Monday, as he would be detained, to assist in the laying of the corner stone of Pisgah A. M. E. Church[99] in erection at Sumter, S. C., and would hold his quarter on Monday, and the Bishop would preach for the people at night. So I had to preach morning and evening to a packed house of appreciative hearers, and, praise the Lord, we had a glorious time. What made it more so was the conversion of an old man who heretofore disdained to go to the church but occupied the time to stroll the roads, but hearing a woman is to preach, (he told this out of his mouth in the church), I thought for curiosity I would come to hear what she would say, and I now at the close of this meeting, I want to tell you all that God has sent this woman to arrest me and bring me out of darkness into light, and I believe to-night that I am a saved man in Jesus by the Gospel as I understand it. Blessed be the name of the Lord. The wretched sinner man claimed to understand enough of God's word to be saved. The many white friends that were present showed their faith in the words as expressed by the saved sinner in returning, and renewed their contributions to the aid of the Missionary. Sermon preached from the loving call of Jesus, "Come unto me, all that are weary and heavy laden, and I will give thee rest to your souls."[100] I announced that I would address the Daughters of Conference at 11 on Monday and wanted all who are out to-day to be present, as the Elder and the Bishop would be here to give the communion, and they were out on time. Surely the people were happy—here they come. I closed up as the Bishop ascended, but he pressed me on, and in his turn he gave us a grand address from the words, "And yet there is room." At the close of his service he announced receiving a dispatch that demanded his return and could not stay to preach at night, and asked for a vote whether or not he should leave me in his place, and the whole assembly rose in yea, yea. Mysterious life, indeed. The poor, weak one to preach in place of our great Bishop, so in obedience, I gave a little lecture on Morality, at night, and left on Tuesday for my quiet little country home, Titled by the sainted little wife of Rev. Frank Crum, nephew to the famous Dr. W. D. Crum, of Charleston, S. C., "Floral Height, R. R. Ave," from its picturesque and floral appearance.

99. Pisgah AME is known as Mt. Pisgah AME and is still in existence at 217 W. Bartlette Street.

100. The sermon title comes from Matthew 11:28-29: "Come unto me, all ye that labour and are heavy laden, and I will give you rest. Take my yoke upon you, and learn of me; for I am meek and lowly in heart: and ye shall find rest unto your souls."

Among my mail I found one of note. As it is only such that gave light on the life and calling of the writer, here it is again, from Rev. C. P. Nelson, D. D., P. E. of the Columbia District,[101] and the Rev. B. F. Witherspoon, P. E. of the M. E. Church.[102] Dr. Nelson enclosed an appointment as Treasurer for Berkeley County, S. C., for the Rolla, North Carolina Exposition. Now hear this, my talented friend and brother, read it.

20 Felix St., Charleston, S. C. Mrs. C. S. Riley, Lincolnville, S. C.

Dearly Beloved in the Lord Jesus Christ: Your most fervent letter of the 30th came duly to hand. The written matter so engaged my attention that the silver was not noticed at all. In fact, it dropped out on the carpet and had not the contents of your letter spoke of it with a request, I should have not known it dropped. The baby would if she could have us thank you. Mother and baby are doing nicely. I suppose you are wondering what the S. S. J. attached by me to your name mean. I will tell you. It means "Soul-Saver through Jesus." Now don't blush. It is all true. If God has ever used a human being in saving the souls of others, he certainly has used you. O, that he may use you more and more. Your sickness was very grievous unto me, and now since you are convalescent, will again and with you rejoice. I have found a full salvation, my beloved in Jesus. I am resting at the cross. I am calmly trusting, every moment now is sweet. I am resting at His feet. Come when you can and see us in our new home. The madam is very fond of you. God bless you.

Yours truly,

B. F. WITHERSPOON.

This is also pleasant to read:

827 Broad St., Providence, R. I.

Dear Mrs. Riley: Your lovely Xmas card to Mrs. J. K. Barney came to hand, and as she is in Europe and will not be home for some time, have laid it

101. Rev. C. P. Nelson is noted as leading prayer on May 24 at the Consecration of Bishops in C. Smith, *History of the African Methodist Episcopal Church*, 156.

102. Rev. Witherspoon is noted as the first financial supporter for the republication of the *Methodist Messenger*, the South Carolina Conference paper. He was born in Columbia, South Carolina, fulfilled his ministry in Anderson, and was noted to be "very successful in the ministry." See Ruliff Vancleve Lawrence and Ellwood Haines Stokes, *The Centenary Souvenir containing a History of Centenary Church, Charleston, and an Account of the Life and Labors of Rev. R. V. Lawrence* (Philadelphia: Collins Printing House, 1885).

carefully away in her desk to welcome her on her return. I know she will greatly appreciate your loving remembrance of her.

Very cordially yours,

HARRIOTTE D. WALKER, Secy.

Hear, hear, the Madam has returned.

Providence, R. I., U. S. A., Supt. and Prison Evangelist.

Dear Mrs. Riley: When your letter came I was far away over the Atlantic and did not return until three weeks ago. Just now I am very much pressed on every side with work which had accumulated in my six months' absence. I shall mail you some copies of our Christian Endeavor for your Society. May God strengthen you for all your labors and spare you many years to be a blessing to those who look to you for spiritual help. Kind remembrance to your dear ones, and believe me, Most sincerely your friend and sister in Christ,

J. K. BARNEY.

My heart goes out in gratitude to my Heavenly Father for the prayer of the righteous. Shall we prevail with God? We have the sainted Bishop James Shorter[103] as presiding over the S. C. Annual Conference at the old Emanuel Church, Charleston, S. C. He transferred me from the Columbia to the S. C. Conference, and since coming down here I simply held the position of Conference Missionary, with all privilege to give service to the churches as my health will allow, and the good pastors will look to my help. However poor my health is, I have tried to do much by precept and example quietly assailing Satan upon every hand, and have much to do at my home church, while indulging myself in the Association, the Holy Spirit." [*sic*] Well, dear reader, rather than boast in my work, let me come to mission and revelation, as the revelation of a vision prove the Spirit's work in the vision of the soul under an attack of illness. At 6 o'clock one winter morning, as I appear to have been out in open air, I hear a peculiar sound, and seeing the moon passing swiftly toward the East, I hailed, "What is that sound I hear?" and the answer came to my question, as from the

---

103. Bishop James A. Shorter (1817–87) was born in Washington, DC. He first joined the Methodist Episcopal Church in 1839 in Galena, Illinois, and later that same year joined the Bethel AME Church in Philadelphia, Pennsylvania, under Bishop Morris Brown. He began his itinerant preaching career in the Baltimore Conference in 1846, served various churches, and was elected the ninth bishop of the AME Church in 1868.

moon, "The sound you hear is God." And I looked up toward the heavens and I saw as the sun in its meridian. And I looked at the sun with great reverence, and in the sun I saw an eye looking down upon me. And with awful apprehension I stood and gazed into the great beautiful eye, and cried aloud to the inhabitants to come and see this beautiful sight. Surely they came though I knew not. As I was as in a trance, all my time was occupied with this eye. I saw in the eye God's anger, God's love, God's mercy, forming the Trinity. Yes, I beheld through this great luminous eye, God's anger for sin, His love for sinners, and His mercy to save, and I was under this peculiar vision for six or seven days. I was not myself. Our pastor Alexander, Ransom, The Rev. Soney J. Brown and many more of God's people visited me expecting me to die, and no one attempted to doubt the vision, but interpreted it to be a singled out work for me to do, and time will reveal the same and all lived to see its revelation. The time did come when Satan had severely assailed our beloved Zion, when everything seemed dark around her for sin had nestled in her sacred walls, and God seemed angry and had drawn himself from us—when the voice of the Elders was not heard, when the enemies laughed in our face. But a change was made. The new pastor came in the spirit of a Moses. The man beloved by all who knew him, the man for peace and Godliness. Yes, this good man, the Rev. Samuel Bellamy, who called the writer up to help rescue our beloved Zion. We thought to organize the noted society, viz: the Christian Endeavor. That may give a little shining out of darkness which has been a great solace to the true in heart, and we struck away from among the pretenders and deceivers in Zion. This society was organized in the name of God and to His glory. It is now seven years old and is still being led on by the writer, who calls upon you to join in the "Glory be to the Father, and to the Son, and to the Holy Ghost." Forever here my rest shall be, "close to the Redeemer's side, and this shall always be my plea, it is for me the blessed Savior died."[104]

Thank the Lord, I have recovered from my illness and am able to take a change of climate and have decided to start on my way for Columbia, the capital city of S. C., trusting that I shall be at rest in body and mind, and have been

---

104. This passage combines the traditional doxology, "Glory be to the Father, and to the Son, and to the Holy Ghost. As it was in the beginning, is now and ever shall be, world without end, Amen," and the first stanza of hymn number 130 in Elisha A. Hoffman, ed., *Christian Endeavor: Echoes and Manual of Services* (Chicago: Hope Publishing, 1895), "Forever here my rest shall be, / Close to thy bleeding side: / This all my hope, and all my plea, / For me the Saviour died."

nicely cared for by my devoted friend, Miss Polly Pickens, the host of the most noted in the city, as most of the noted preachers board there with other professional men and women. But one week to-day I was here composing myself in ease and enjoying the association of the learned and wise men and women of the race. Here comes the mail man with an official envelope. I hastily opened it, to find it to be a recommendation signed by the citizens of the Hill to have me insert my name, accepting the petition, and send it to Washington, D. C., P. O. Department, as the post master, Miss Catherine Wallace, saw fit to resign, having to rent and not sufficient in the fourth class office to pay her expenses, and as an excellent teacher, she accepted a position as teacher for a school that would pay her to advantage in the city of Texas, with her good luck to stop with the sweet wife of our beloved Bishop A. Grant,[105] and this excellent young lady recommended the writer to the department on her resignation as the one to succeed her, and this is the petition I sent up on Tuesday, the day after received, and to my astonishment Dr. John J. Durham brought me the paper announcing my appointment on Sunday morning. Well, I held all was right, as I had my adopted son, David Riley Hill at school to this dear lady friend of ours and P. M., so he understood much about the business, and being a very intelligent, bright lad, he could be my clerk in the business, as I would be obliged to have a clerk to hang the pouch, as it would be too much for me to do. I arrived at home in time to have my bond by the polished and successful gentleman, Mr. Frank Hoffman, of Summerville, S. C., and my commission came the last day of Sept., and the P. M. turned over the office to me at six o'clock in the morning, and she took the train at eight o'clock of the same p. m. for her new home. So my obligation began on the first day of October, 1885.[106] My son David was of great value to me for he was under my dictation and control. He was as solid in business of every kind as gold. I had to give him up after his graduation at Avery Institute at Charleston, S. C., and having to support himself, he had to leave home, as he could not be recompensed out of the business of the office, for there is not enough for one of us, and he has been teaching ever since he left school with his sheepscoat. So my daughter, who never can or will leave me alone at any time, is still at my side truthfully and trustily trudging with me in

105. Bishop Abraham Grant (1848–1911) was the nineteenth bishop elected to the AME Church.

106. Riley was appointed on August 20, 1885, and took the oath on September 8; the Postmaster General sealed the appointment on September 16, and she assumed her responsibilities on October 1.

the tedious service of Uncle Sam. During the dreadful earthquake of 1886, that Charleston and its surroundings ought never to forget, when men, women and children, even the beasts of the forest, were trying to run away from God's wondrous work, the surrounding scene of terror and alarm, and deprived of their Moses to guide them, the writer as the lesser light, though supported by crutches on account of lameness, was sought for and pressed to come to the place they gathered at, and dispense to them God's sure words of promise, as spoken by Jehovah.[107] Many accepted the message of the Lord and were saved by faith, believing that Jesus, the Friend of sinners, can and will save. With Christian pride I am able to tell you my son was among the number that claimed saving faith in the Lord Jesus. He is now a man and is still following the army. My daughter is a strong worker in the church of God. However tedious we may find the journey and troublesome may be the way, with God on our side, "we are faint yet pursuing on the journey to victory."[108] The honor of being among Uncle Sam's boys in the office is only an accommodation for the people, as is the most in it, and thus employed does not hinder the gleaner to follow after the reapers, and need not be idle, as the doors of all the churches irrespective are open to my acceptance. It was my good fortune to have been at home and was able to attend divine service on the second Sabbath of May, and heard the sermon preached by the Rev. C. W. McQueen, selected from Second Cor. 12: 1, and so vividly expounded the same to the minds of those who were prepared to receive.[109] The preacher could never know how much he had

107. The seismic history of the southeastern United States is dominated by the 1886 earthquake that occurred near Charleston, South Carolina. It was one of the largest recorded earthquakes in eastern North America and by far the largest earthquake in the southeastern United States. The major shock occurred on August 31, 1886, at approximately 9:50 p.m. Although it lasted less than one minute, there was extensive damage to the city of Charleston, and about sixty people died. Moreover, of the 435 or more earthquakes reported to have taken place in South Carolina between 1754 and 1975, more than 300 were aftershocks that occurred in the first thirty-five years following 1886. See http://www.seis.sc.edu/projects /SCSN/history/html/eqchas.html.

108. A reference to the Old Testament judge Gideon's leadership against the Midianites in Judges 7:7–9; 8:4.

109. 2 Corinthians 12.1: "It is not expedient for me doubtless to glory. I will come to visions and revelations of the Lord." Paul was caught up into the third heaven and subsequently received a "thorn" in his flesh to keep him humble because of the numerous revelations he had experienced.

confirmed me in my illustration on one of the events and mystery in the little book until he shall have read the same, as he imparted to his hearers "in Paul to save himself from the appearance of egotism." He took up as a defence [*sic*] the vision of his spirit and the revelation of the vision, — this experimental knowledge, said Paul, boasting in himself. However, he had all liberty to boast in the great work he has done. He saw best to turn the high uplifting of his spiritual life to God alone so the world may see the reality and favor of God toward those who trust Him for His grace which is sufficient in all time and in eternity. The Rev. was grand all through the lesson. And why should I be less than Paul in my faith in the vision of my soul; that God, who is no respecter of persons, would do less for me than he has done for Paul? Would you attempt to dispute the Spirit's work that it answers not to flesh and blood, but answers Spirit to Spirit? The Rev. McQueen understood this, for could you have heard his diction as I did, you would have concluded that he is truly an expounder of the words of truth. Now, here is my commission from Uncle Sam, an honor unsought for, which seals the title of the book. You may like to hear it, as it reads:

William F. Vilas, Postmaster General of the United States of America.[110]

To all to whom these presents shall come, Greeting:

Whereas on the 20th day of August, 1885, Mrs. Charlotte S. Riley was appointed post master at Lincolnville, in the County of Berkeley, State of S. C., and whereas she did, on the 8th day of Sept., 1885, execute a bond, and has taken the oath of office, as required by law: Now, know ye, that confiding in the integrity, ability and punctuality of the said Mrs. Charlotte S. Riley, I do commission her a post master authorized to execute the duties of that office at Lincolnville aforesaid, according to the laws of the United States, and the regulations of the Post Office Department. To hold the said office of postmaster, with all the power, privileges and emoluments to the same belonging, during the pleasure of the Postmaster General of the United States. In testimony wherein, I have herein set my hand and caused the seal of the Post Office Department to be affixed, at Washington City, this sixteenth day of Sept., in

110. William F. Vilas, Postmaster General (1840–1908), was born in Vermont but moved with his parents to Wisconsin. He enlisted in the Union Army during the Civil War and later became both a law professor at the University of Wisconsin and a US senator. He was appointed postmaster general of the United States under President Grover Cleveland from 1885 to 1888 and then became secretary of the interior of the United States.

the year of our Lord, 1885, and of the independence of the United States the
one hundred and tenth.

WILLIAM F. VILAS,
Postmaster General.

Now I sing, "All glory and praise to the God of all grace, who has bought
us, and sought us, and guided our ways. Hallelujah, Thine the glory, Amen."[111]
Do you see what the providence of God has given to his poor, afflicted child?
Surely He careth for His own.

The mail has come and I am anxious to have mine. They are always of
great importance and solace to me. Whose is this? O, from my dear boy. Let us
hear what he shall say to his mother.

St. Stephen's Church, Wilmington, N. C.[112]

Dear Mother, Mrs. C. S. Riley: I was indeed sorry to learn of your long and
serious illness. Truly you are a child of affliction. I can see nothing in it but a
Divine purpose. O, that you may continue to rely entirely upon Him for supporting you. The St. Stephen's Church is a mill that grinds from daily dawn to
midnight. God is crowning our labors. The more I know the people the better I
like them. I send you a copy of our monthly statement. We have commenced
the erection of a steeple at the cost of fifteen hundred and fifty-eight dollars. I
hope to have you with us soon, say some time this summer, God willing. Shall
say more in my next. Yours in unchanged affection,

　　Your son in Christ,

E. J. GREGG.

Let us see the other. Well, well, this is a long-lost friend.

Chattanooga, Tenn.

Dear Madam: I was more than glad to hear of you. It certainly recalls to
my mind the memory of the good old days spent with you in Sunday school and
church. Happy am I to hear from you, and to remember that you taught me to

---

111. This is the third stanza of the hymn "Revive Us Again," words by William MacKay
(1863) and music by John Husband (1815).

112. While there are two existing churches of this name in Wilmington, North Carolina,
it is likely the one located at 501 Redcross Street; see http://www.ncmarkers.com/Markers
.aspx?MarkerId=D-77.

work in wisdom's path. Many times I am made to think of you, and St. Peter's Church. I only ask you to pray for me and speak to the young men and women about our College, as I believe a brighter future awaits the school. I am still in the loyal rank of Tennessee volunteers of the grand old A. M. E. church, laboring for the Master, and have all ready packed up for at any time to take homeward bound train. Bye, bye.

Yours truly,

T. W. HAIGLER, M. D., Dean.[113]
Professor of Materia Medica, Surgery and Pathology.

These are the things that never die. As one has said, "the tired hand stretched forth to aid a brother in his time of need, a kindly word in grief's dark hour that proves a friend indeed." The plea for mercy softly breathed when Justice threatens nigh, the sorrow of a contrite, grateful heart, are things that never die.[114]

You see at once that these letters were kept as souvenirs and see how well they fit in the building up of character. "I am so glad for the Book that is given, tells of the love of our Father in Heaven, but of all the glorious things in the Book we do see, the greatest of all is that Jesus loves me."[115] Let us read all of

113. T. W. Haigler, MD, dean and professor of materia medica (now termed "pharmacology"), surgery, and pathology at Chattanooga Medical College. Chattanooga Medical College was founded in 1889 but closed in 1910; the historically black Chattanooga National Medical College was founded in 1899 but closed in 1904. (A picture, ca. 1907, exists of him listing him in Nashville, Tennessee, and the pastor of St. John AME Church.)

114. Quoted from the second stanza of the poem "Things that Never Die," by Charles Dickens (1812–70): "The pure, the bright, the beautiful / that stirred our hearts in youth, / The impulses to wordless prayer, / The streams of love and truth, / The longing after something lost, / The spirit's longing cry, / The striving after better hopes—/ These things can never die. / The timid hand stretched forth to aid / A brother in his need; / A kindly word in grief's dark hour / That proves a friend indeed; / The plea for mercy softly breathed, / When justice threatens high, / The sorrow of a contrite heart—/ These things shall never die. / Let nothing pass, for every hand / Must find some work to do, / Lose not a chance to waken love—/ Be firm and just and true. / So shall a light that cannot fade / Beam on thee from on high, / And angel voices say to thee—/ 'These things shall never die.'"

115. A quotation from the first stanza of the hymn "Jesus Loves Even Me," words and music by Philip Bliss (1870): "I am so glad that our Father in Heav'n / Tells of His love in the Book He has giv'n; / Wonderful things in the Bible I see, / This is the dearest, that Jesus loves me."

the letters. Here is one from my son David Riley Hill, New York. I give you as he wrote in my household name.

> Dear Darling:
> I visited Brooklyn to-day, Sunday, p. m. I stopped in to see Rev. John S. Brown at his residence, 17 Rockwell Place. As I struck the doorstep he asked if that was his little son David, of the one who attended the door. He said "let him come." I did not intend going in for the pastor of Fleet Street Church had begged his people not to visit him as he was extremely weak, but he must see his mother's son. I obeyed and he said: "I want to tell you to say to Mother Riley that I have not forgotten her words when leaving the South. Tell her I have kept her words of comfort, tell her the words 'My son, go, and God will be with you' are still in my mind. Tell her God is with me now and will be with me to the end," then he wept and said "tell her good-by." And I left the room.

Glory to God, he is safe in the promised land. Very good, yes. "This is my story, this is my song, to praise my Redeemer all the day long."[116] Indeed my experience in the journeys of life, "upon the mountain high and in the valley low, and in the burning sun of affliction, and the beating rain of persecution, in the gulf of despondency, and the frost of spiritual coldness around us, has done much to hasten the dissolving of my building." "But when it shall be dissolved, I shall have a building not made with hands, but eternal and on high," — 2 Cor. 5: 1.[117] I am still here, however, in this great battle of life, "until the war is ended." Physically worn, but having on the uniform and fully equipped, I shall keep in rank on all side."

Well, hold on, I have a letter to mail. You may like to hear and I want you to hear the venture in the Christian liberty.

116. Quoted from the hymn "Blessed Assurance," words and music by Fanny Crosby (1873): "Blessed assurance, Jesus is mine! O what a foretaste of glory divine! Heir of salvation, purchase of God, Born of His Spirit, washed in His blood. / This is my story, this is my song, Praising my Savior, all the day long; This is my story, this is my song, Praising my Savior, all the day long.

117. 2 Corinthians 5:1: "For we know that if our earthly house of this tabernacle were dissolved, we have a building of God, an house not made with hands, eternal in the heavens."

Lincolnville, S. C.

To the President of the United States, Greeting:

Dear Sir: Learning that you are to visit the Charleston Exposition,[118] I write my desire with the patrons of this Postoffice, more especially the ladies, that on passing office situated on the South Carolina R. R., twenty miles of Charleston that you will have your train slow by that we may behold your god-like person, as we are unable to see our President otherwise.

Most respectfully,

CHARLOTTE S. RILEY,
Postmaster Lincolnville, S. C.

Did you get an answer for sure? You might know that Mr. Theodore Roosevelt is a man after "God's own mind." Hear it.

No. 1075. Office of the Fourth Assistant Postmaster General, Appointment Division, Washington, D. C.

Sir: Your communication of the 7th on the subject of the P. O. at Lincolnville, S. C., addressed to the President, has by his direction, been forwarded to this department for acknowledgment. I have to advise you that the same has been filed and will receive consideration when the case is taken up for action.

Very truly yours,

J. K. BRISTOW,
Third Assistant P. M. General.

Did you see him on the trip? Indeed, the godly man appeared out upon the rear platform with his aides and doffed his handsome silk beaver to the assembled patrons under the stars and stripes, as far as we could see the godly and manly man.[119] Then we sang the song written by the P. M. on Emancipation day. You may like to hear it. "Who, who are these assembled here to-day?

118. The World's Fair, formally named the South Carolina Interstate and West Indian Exposition, was held in Charleston, South Carolina, in 1901–2.

119. According to Charleston's newspaper, *Post and Courier*, President Theodore Roosevelt (1858–1919) arrived in Charleston on April 8, 1902, the first president to visit the area since before the Civil War. During his two-day visit, he took a side trip to Summerville, the larger community of Lincolnville. See "Good Morning Lowcountry," *Post and Courier*, April 8, 2002, 2B.

They are those who were oppressed slaves, but they trusted in their God, and now at liberty. Then through the war of right against the wrong they fought for liberty. Yes, these are they who through slavery dire boldly and true have stood the hottest fire, hoping onward to rise higher, trusting for liberty."

Dear reader, I note you these events as the index that points out to the eventful life of the writer. After the old Emanuel had been completed, the women of the church were called to have her decorated and adorned for dedication, and they met to do her honor. In arranging the floral designs, the writer ascended the pulpit and opened the beautiful claret colored Bible and called for attention to my song, when one of my friends called me to come down, saying, "When that comes to pass, the world will come to an end." But in this we see how far God's ways are from man's, and how high is his thought above ours," [*sic*][120] for that sister is alive to-day that have witnessed the preacher in the same pulpit and heard her discourse from the same Bible, and she shouted to the glory of God with the multitude on a communion Sabbath morning, under the kindness of the Rev. W. W. Beckill, D. D., then pastor of the church, now the P. E. of Charleston district, the progressive theologian, as in his expressive sermons, the writer "predicted his ascension to the Bishopric." Why not for one who has so many elective admirers? I believe all of this, and my friend has not seen the end of the world yet. Gathering up the fragments of flowers after the decoration of Emanuel, I put up a tiny bouquet of a little rosebud and fern lines, and put it in my Bible to press as a souvenir, and after the lapse of twenty years, the Rev. Wm. Beamer, pastor of Summerville circuit, called on me to inform me the program he presents me is the quarto-centenary of the African Methodist Episcopal Church established in this Southland at the close of the war, and that I shall be called upon to make an address on Saturday, set apart as the women's day, and that the renowned elocutionist, Miss H. A. Brown, will be in the lead of the woman's talk. The program read on this wise: Saturday, three p. m., devotional exercise, conducted by Rev. Mrs. C. S. Riley. Subject of Miss Brown, "What shall we do with our girls?" with a general discussion by the ladies of the church, but I found myself the only woman present to follow after Miss Brown. O, how glad I found the little, almost forgotten pressed bouquet, and took it out for display with a little composition on its presence

120. A reference to Isaiah 55:8–9: "For my thoughts are not your thoughts, neither are your ways my ways, saith the Lord. For as the heavens are higher than the earth, so are my ways higher than your ways, and my thoughts than your thoughts."

and read "This is written on a bouquet preserved from the decoration of this church in 1866." This is a treasure dear, a souvenir of twenty years. This bunch of pressed flowers, there is a charm among these faded leaves that binds the past years to this Quarto-Centenary day. We little thought when plucked from yonder pulpit vase and put to press, that this would be thy review, treasured bouquet. What cause to pluck the flowers from gardens fair by busy hands and eager hearts? It was to adorn your pulpit stand in honor of the sainted one who came to gather Afric's sons. Africanism was the holy cry. Men ran to here from everywhere. Then the war for right began. Opposed they were on every side, but the God of truth and right brought them victory by His might. This Quarto-Centenary day awaken our minds to the first alarm given by the "God-sent man." This was the theme: "Come all ye blind to Christ and see; come all ye bond and be made free, to praise God under our own fig tree." So they came from far and near, and every one was Afric's sable son. They built their house at His command, and firm with Him they all did stand. Then sounded out through the Southland, the Great Emanuel is complete. The battle fought, the victory won, and the applauds went down the line, God bless our Cain. With Afric's sons, these faded flowers join us in response to words of praise. Though that form in dust is laid, dear friend, we miss thee now, thy skillful hand and anxious brow, thy tongue of wisdom,—busy brain, how sweet to memory is thy name. Thy useful talent, power and wit, but in God's Holy Book 'tis writ, and the glory for to be we will read it in eternity. Of the army firm and strong, with this banner hoisted high, Africanism shall never die, until they join the host, the blood-washed choir, with Bishop Allen, the Bush on fire, and Elder Carr, the sainted sire, the heavenly fire man, Old Man Graham, with many more that shall be known, shall "Sing forever around God's great white throne."[121] These are examples and labors that should never pass from our minds, as pointers for

---

121. The timeline here needs clarification. Riley sang her Emancipation Day song during Roosevelt's visit in April 1902 and then remembers that she had sung it at the building dedication of Emanuel AME in Charleston in 1872. At that time, she gathered fragments of flowers from the decorations and made a bouquet and pressed it in her Bible. Twenty years later, in 1891, the Rev. William Beamer, pastor of Summerville circuit, informed her that she would be the Saturday speaker at the quarto-centenary celebration of the 1866 establishment of the AME Church in the south. Since the term "quarto-centenary" refers to a 400-year anniversary, she must be using the term to reference the church's twenty-fifth anniversary, which also included the dedication of Emanuel's newest edifice. For the history of Emanuel AME Church, see note 26.

our turn in the race of life. No, the laborers' work of success and faith may beam in our soul with the whisper of the angel in our mind. These things shall never die. Let it be kept for others' good. Many curious minds have been made to accept grand lessons from a simple word. "Jesus said unto the curious Zaccheus the simple words this day: Salvation abide at your house, and the simple announcement made him a changed man."[122] You may take these announcements as said of the writer. Mr. Editor,[123] all hail New Year's day in celebrating the event of Freedom. Mr. Sydney Woodward, now sojourning in Charleston, has been spending the week here in preparation for a concert at the Opera House, Summerville, S. C. While here the noted singer has been entertained by Mrs. C. S. Riley, our distinguished postmistress, who is known for her generous hospitality. Many noted guests were present, our most excellent Dr. J. H. Alston and Mr. Frank Springs of Summerville, S. C., Mrs. G. A. Albright is here again. At a large meeting held on Monday evening for the organizing an Educational Association. The following officers were elected: Pres., W. H. Washington; Vice Pres., Rev. Buffit; Sec., Miss M. E. Seabrook; Treasurer, Rev. Mrs. C. S. Riley. So it comes. There is the advertisements. Good news from the Orphan Industrial Farm and the Scott's Industrial School. The following are the names of the managers who will conduct the farm another year: Rev. D. J. Jenkins, Pres. F. W. Hoffman, Dr. W. D. Crum, W. H. Johnson, Rev. Mrs. C. S. Riley, Rev. J. A. Seal, E. R. Ayer, Wm. H. Washington. F. P. Crum has been elected superintendent. This is the Board, among the leading citizens of the State of South Carolina: Pub. *Charleston Messenger.* . . .   .

122. A reference to Jesus's interaction with Zacchaeus, the publican, in Luke 19:9: "And Jesus said unto him, This day is salvation come to this house, forsomuch as he also is a son of Abraham."

123. Daniel Joseph Jenkins (1853–1937), pastor and business owner who founded the Orphan Aid Society and later the Orphan Industrial Farm, which became known as the Jenkins Orphanage Institute. During his lifetime, the institute provided shelter and training to over 5,000 boys and girls. Jenkins organized some of the children into a band that helped raise money for and brought notoriety to the organization. The band played at the inaugural parades of both Presidents Theodore Roosevelt (1905) and William Taft (1909). To support the institute, Jenkins also purchased a printing press, publishing works by local authors, including Charlotte Riley, and a weekly newspaper, the *Charleston Messenger*. For more on Jenkins, see Walter J. Frazer, *Charleston! Charleston! The History of a Southern City* (Columbia: University of South Carolina Press, 1989); and Lynn Abbott and Doug Seroff, *Out of Sight: The Rise of African American Popular Music, 1889–1895* (Jackson: University Press of Mississippi, 2002). See also http://www.jenkinsinstitute.org.

Mr. Editor: This is to the Rev. D. J. Jenkins. Dear Brother, through the vigilant command of the A. Y. P. C. E., the Rev. C. S. Riley the small sum of one dollar was collected on last Sunday in consent of the same by its members. It is sent to you in aid of the Orphan's Thanksgiving dinner. We know it is a very small help, but we believe on the day of reckoning small duties that are neglected shall be called up to be accounted for before the Great Judge of all things, and in this we hope we will not be found among the sorry number, see?

G. A. ALBRIGHT.

Clippings after the rousing address of the orator of the day, the Rev. Caroll, of Columbia, S. C.

Rev. J. L. McCoy introduced the Rev. Mrs. C. S. Riley, of Lincolnville, S. C., as being one of the greatest powers in society among women, and the only woman preacher in South Carolina. Mrs. Riley is the strongest and most forcible lady orator that has ever appeared before an audience in this State. She started by reviewing the work of Rev. D. J. Jenkins, President of the Orphan Aid Society, which has done so much for the poor colored children, and ending by predicting that in the future the Scott's High School and Industrial Farm will revolutionize the status of the negro. Every one present paid strict attention to all that was said by Rev. Mrs. Riley, and on all sides could be heard in that vast crowd expressions of praises to her strong words of commendation and advice, and all pronounced hers as the most interesting speech of the day. We hope to have the Rev. lady come to Charleston in the near future and deliver an address for the benefit of the Orphans.

Another clipping on the same.

Mrs. Rev. Riley is a ready power and woman orator. Her address at Ladson, S. C., with her right finger directed to the Scotts building, was wonderful. She captured the multitude of people for fifteen minutes. She is a woman of to-day. More on Mrs. Riley's order are needed in South Carolina.

Blessed be the name of the Lord, for the little good I may be able to accomplish and you may think or charge me as an egotist. Think well, reader, before you express it. Can't you see I am entirely out of the case? I am only making you out the repetition of others, and this is the order of the book. And you promised your kindest feeling and clearest judgment. And I can't afford to let these high appreciations of my little labors be lost. O, no, they can, nor shall never die as long as a page of the little book on the Mysterious Life and Calling remains. Are you tired? Well, it is written among the rest. How can your mind rest before you hear it all?

> The Rev. Mrs. Riley organized a C. E. S.[124] at Lincolnville, S. C., which has been the means of developing the Christian and general status of the town, the membership growing rapidly each year. In 1885 she received the appointment of Postmaster at Lincolnville, and has made an efficient officer, with a record surpassing many in such places. Mrs. Riley's home is on an acre of land, nicely cultivated, her flower garden, with its numerous shrubs, roses and flowers, too numerous to mention, is the pride of her heart. She calls them God's messengers of love. Her doors are always open to strangers, as well as friends, and all made happy under her hospitable domain—(From the Headlight, of Summerville, S. C.)

You shall have the balance of this life when the writer shall have moved away out of time.

Now, whenever, and whoever shall read the contents of this little book, this that is written within, shall be known as it is known[125] and held in remembrance and reverence of her labors of love and mercy toward her fellow-man, through a mysterious life and calling.

Written and dedicated to the help of her declining years.

> "Help us to help each other,
> Each other's cross to bear,
> And when the glory crown shall be given,
> We all shall have our share."

Then we shall join in the Coronation Song, and "Crown Him Lord of All."[126] Amen.

124. Christian Education Society.

125. A reference to 1 Corinthians 13:12: "For now we see through a glass, darkly; but then face to face: now I know in part; but then shall I know even as also I am known."

126. These words are from the hymn commonly known as "All Hail the Power of Jesus' Name," words by Edward Perronet (1789) and music by Oliver Holden (1793); it is actually titled "Coronation": "All hail the power of Jesus' Name! / Let angels prostrate fall; / Bring forth the royal diadem, / and crown Him Lord of all. / Bring forth the royal diadem, / and crown Him Lord of all."

BIBLIOGRAPHY

Abbott, Lynn, and Doug Seroff. *Out of Sight: The Rise of African American Popular Music, 1889–1895.* Jackson: University Press of Mississippi, 2002.

Abbott, Martin. "The Freedman's Bureau and Negro Schooling in South Carolina." *South Carolina Historical Magazine* 57 (April 1956): 65–81.

Acornley, John H. *The Colored Lady Evangelist: Being the Life, Labors, and Experiences of Mrs. Harriet A. Baker.* Brooklyn: n.p., 1892.

Anderson, James D. *The Education of Blacks in the South, 1860–1935.* Chapel Hill: University of North Carolina Press, 1988.

Angelou, Maya. *The Collected Autobiographies of Maya Angelou.* New York: Modern Library, 2004.

———. *I Know Why the Caged Bird Sings.* New York: Random House, 2015.

Andrews, William, ed. *Sisters of the Spirit: Three Black Women's Autobiographies of the Nineteenth Century.* Bloomington: Indiana University Press, 1986.

Ashton, Susanna, ed. *I Belong to South Carolina: South Carolina Slave Narratives.* Columbia: University of South Carolina Press, 2010.

Ashton, Susanna, and Rhondda Robinson Thomas, eds. *The South Carolina Roots of African American Thought: A Reader.* Columbia: University of South Carolina Press, 2014.

Ball, Edward. *Slaves in the Family.* New York: Ballantine, 1999.

Barthelemy, Anthony, ed. *Collected Black Women's Narratives.* The Schomburg Library of Nineteenth-Century Black Women Writers. New York: Oxford University Press, 1988.

Bassard, Katherine Clay. "Gender and Genre: Black Women's Autobiography and the Ideology of Literacy." *African American Review* 26, no. 1 (Spring 1992): 119–29.

———. *Spiritual Interrogations: Culture, Gender, and Community in Early African American Women Writers.* Princeton, NJ: Princeton University Press, 1999.

Beecher, Henry Ward. *Star Papers: Or, Experiences of Art and Nature.* Bedford, MA: Applewood Books, 1855.

Berlin, Ira. *Generations of Captivity: A History of African American Slaves.* Cambridge, MA: Harvard University Press, 2003.

Birnie, C. W. "Education of the Negro in Charleston, South Carolina Prior to the Civil War." *Journal of Negro History* 12 (January 1927): 13–21.

Blackman, Douglas A. *Slavery by Another Name: The Re-Enslavement of Black Americans from the Civil War to World War II*. New York: Anchor Books, 2008.

Braxton, Joanne. *Black Women Writing Autobiography: A Tradition within a Tradition*. Philadelphia: Temple University Press, 1989.

Bunch-Lyons, Beverly. "John Mifflin Brown." In *Slavery in the United States: A Social, Political, and Historical Encyclopedia*, edited by Junius P. Rodriguez, 207–8. Santa Barbara: ABC-CLIO, 2007.

Carillo, Karen Juanita. *African American History Day by Day: A Reference Guide to Events*. Santa Barbara: Greenwood, 2012.

Cassedy, James Gilbert. "African Americans and the American Labor Movement." *Prologue Magazine* 29, no. 2 (Summer 1997). http://www.archives.gov/publications /prologue/1997/summer/american-labor-movement.html.

Collier-Thomas, Bettye. *Daughters of Thunder: Black Women Preachers and Their Sermons, 1850–1979*. San Francisco: Jossey-Bass, 1998.

Coppin, Fannie Jackson. "In Memory of Bishop Jabez Pitt Campbell." *A.M.E. Church Review* 8, no. 2 (October 1891): 152–53.

Crafts, Hannah. *The Bondwoman's Narrative*. Edited by Henry Louis Gates Jr. New York: Warner Books, 2002.

Culp, D. W., ed. *Twentieth Century Negro Literature, or, A Cyclopedia of Thought on the Vital Topics Relating to the American Negro by One Hundred of America's Greatest Negroes*. Atlanta: J. L. Nichols, 1902.

Curl, John. *For All the People: Uncovering the Hidden History of Cooperation, Cooperative Movements, and Communalism in America*. Oakland: PM Press, 2012.

·Douglass-Chin, Richard J. *Preacher Woman Sings the Blues: The Autobiographies of Nineteenth-Century African American Evangelists*. Columbia: University of Missouri Press, 2001.

Drago, Edmund L., and Eugene C. Hunt. *A History of Avery Normal Institute from 1865 to 1954*. Rev. and enlarged ed. Charleston: Avery Research Center, 1991.

duCille, Ann. *The Coupling Convention: Sex, Text, and Tradition in Black Women's Fiction*. New York: Oxford University Press, 1993.

Edgar, Walter. *South Carolina: A History*. Columbia: University of South Carolina Press, 1998.

Edwards, Tryon, ed. *A Dictionary of Thoughts Being a Cyclopedia of Laconic Quotations from the Best Authors of the World, Both Ancient and Modern*. New York: Cassell, 1891.

Elrod, Eileen Razzari. *Piety and Dissent: Race, Gender, and Biblical Rhetoric in Early American Autobiography*. Amherst: University of Massachusetts Press, 2008.

Embry, Rev. James C. *Doctrine and Discipline of the African Methodist Episcopal Church*. 18th rev. ed. Philadelphia: AME Book Concern, 1885.

Ernest, John. *Chaotic Justice: Rethinking African American Literary History*. Chapel Hill: University of North Carolina Press, 2009.

———. *Liberation Historiography: African American Writers and the Challenge of History, 1794–1861*. Chapel Hill: University of North Carolina Press, 2004.

Escott, Paul D., et al., eds. *Major Problems in the History of the American South*. Vol. 2, *The New South*. 2nd ed. Boston: Houghton Mifflin, 1999.

Fields, Barbara Jeanne. *Slavery and Freedom on the Middle Ground: Maryland during the Nineteenth Century*. New Haven, CT: Yale University Press, 1985.

Foner, Eric. *Freedom's Lawmakers: A Directory of Black Officeholders during Reconstruction*. New York: Oxford University Press, 1993.

———. *Reconstruction: America's Unfinished Revolution, 1863–1877*. New York: Harper & Row, 1988.

Foster, Frances Smith. *Written by Herself: Literary Production by African American Women, 1746–1892*. Bloomington: Indiana University Press, 1993.

Frazer, Walter J. *Charleston! Charleston! The History of a Southern City*. Columbia: University of South Carolina Press, 1989.

Goodell, William. *The American Slave Code in Theory and Practice: Its Distinctive Features Shown by Its Statutes, Judicial Decisions, and Illustrative Facts*. 3rd ed. New York: American and Foreign Anti-Slavery Society, 1853.

Gijswijt-Hofstra, Marijke. "Neurasthenia." In *Encyclopedia of Disability*, vol. 3, edited by Gary L. Albrecht, 1139–40. Thousand Oaks, CA: Sage Reference, 2006.

Griffin, Farah Jasmine, ed. *Beloved Sisters and Loving Friends*. New York: Ballantine Books, 2001.

Hampton, Christine W., and Rosalee W. Washington. *The History of Lincolnville, South Carolina*. Charleston: BookSurge, 2007.

Harper, Frances Ellen Watkins. *Iola Leroy, or, Shadows Uplifted*. Edited by Hollis Robbins. Penguin Classics. New York: Penguin Books, 2010.

Haywood, Chanta M. *Prophesying Daughters: Black Women Preachers and the Word, 1823–1913*. Columbia: University of Missouri Press, 2003.

Herndl, Diane Price. "The Invisible (Invalid) Woman: African-American Women, Illness and Nineteenth-Century Narrative." *Women's Studies* 24 (1995): 553–72.

Higginbotham, Evelyn Brooks. *Righteous Discontent: The Women's Movement in the Black Baptist Church, 1880–1920*. Cambridge, MA: Harvard University Press, 1993.

Hine, Darlene Clark, ed. *Black Women in America*. 2nd ed. New York: Oxford University Press, 2005.

Hine, William C. "Cain, Richard Harvey." In *American National Biography*, vol. 4, edited by Lewis Burnett-Clarke. New York: Oxford University Press, 1999.

Hoffman, Elisha A., ed., *Christian Endeavor: Echoes and Manual of Services*. Chicago: Hope Publishing, 1895.

Holt, Thomas. *Black over White: Negro Political Leadership in South Carolina during Reconstruction*. Urbana: University of Illinois Press, 1979.

Humez, Jean, ed. *The Writings of Rebecca Jackson: Black Visionary, Shaker Eldress*. Amherst: University of Massachusetts Press, 1987.

Hunter, Jane Edna. *A Nickel and a Prayer: The Autobiography of Jane Edna Hunter*. Edited by Rhondda Robinson Thomas. Regenerations: African American Literature and Culture. Morgantown: West Virginia University Press, 2011.

Jacobs, Harriet. *Incidents in the Life of a Slave Girl Written by Herself.* Edited and with an intro-
    duction by Jean Fagan Yellin. Cambridge, MA: Harvard University Press, 1987.

Jordan, Laylon W. "Education for Community: C. G. Memminger and the Origination
    of Common Schools in Antebellum Charleston." *South Carolina Historical Magazine*
    83 (April 1982): 99–115.

Lawrence, Ruliff Vancleve, and Ellwood Haines Stokes. *The Centenary Souvenir Containing
    a History of Centenary Church, Charleston, and an Account of the Life and Labors of Rev. R. V.
    Lawrence.* Philadelphia: Collins Printing House, 1885.

Lears, Jackson. *Rebirth of a Nation: The Making of Modern America, 1877–1920.* New York:
    HarperCollins, 2009.

Lee, Cindy. *A Tour of Historic Sullivan's Island.* Charleston, SC: History Press, 2010.

Lucas, Marion Brunson. *A History of Blacks in Kentucky: From Slavery to Segregation, 1760–
    1891.* Louisville: Kentucky Historical Society, 2003.

Madigan, Tim. *The Burning: Massacre, Destruction, and Tulsa Race Riot of 1921.* New York:
    St. Martin's Press, 2001.

May, Cedrick. *Evangelism and Resistance in the Black Atlantic, 1760–1835.* Athens: University
    of Georgia Press, 2008.

McKay, Nellie. "Nineteenth-Century Black Women's Spiritual Autobiographies: Reli-
    gious Faith and Self-Empowerment." In *Interpreting Women's Lives: Feminist Theory and
    Personal Narratives,* edited by the Personal Narratives Group, 139–54. Bloomington:
    Indiana University Press, 1989.

McTavish, Jan R. "The Headache in American Medical Practice in the 19th Century:
    A Historical Overview." *Headache: The Journal of Head and Face Pain* 39, no. 4 (April
    1999): 287–98.

Moody, Joycelyn. *Sentimental Confessions: Spiritual Narratives of Nineteenth-Century African
    American Women.* Athens: University of Georgia Press, 2001.

Morris, Robert V., and Julius W. Becton. *Black Faces of War: A Legacy of Honor from the
    American Revolution to Today.* Minneapolis: Zenith Press, 2011.

Morrison, Toni. *The Bluest Eye: A Novel.* 1st Vintage International ed. New York: Vintage
    International, 2007.

"Neurasthenia." In *A Dictionary of Psychology,* edited by Andrew M. Colman. 2nd ed.
    Oxford: Oxford University Press, 2008.

Painter, Nell Irvin. *Exodusters: Black Migration to Kansas after Reconstruction.* New York:
    W. W. Norton, 1986.

———. *Sojourner Truth: A Life, a Symbol.* New York: W. W. Norton, 1996.

Peterson, Carla. *"Doers of the Word": African American Women Speakers and Writers in the North
    (1830–1880).* New York: Oxford University Press, 1995.

Porter, Rose, ed. *Well-Springs of Wisdom: From the Writings of Frederick W. Robertson.* Boston:
    D. Lothrop Company, 1889.

Powers, Bernard E., Jr. *Black Charlestonians: A Social History, 1822–1885.* Fayetteville: Univer-
    sity of Arkansas Press, 1994.

Prioleau, George W. "Is the Chaplain's Work in the Army a Necessity?" In *Active Service, or, Gospel Work among U.S. Soldiers,* edited by Theophilus G. Steward. New York: US Army Aid Association, ca. 1896.

Richardson, Marilyn, ed. *Maria W. Stewart, America's First Black Woman Political Writer.* Bloomington: Indiana University Press, 1987.

Schubert, Frank N. *Voices of the Buffalo Soldier: Records, Reports, and Recollections of Military Life and Service in the West.* Albuquerque: University of New Mexico Press, 2009.

Seraile, William. *Fire in His Heart: Bishop Benjamin Tucker Tanner and the A.M.E. Church.* Knoxville: University of Tennessee Press, 1999.

Sernett, Milton C. *Bound for the Promised Land: African American Religion and the Great Migration.* Durham: Duke University Press, 1997.

Shellum, Brian G. *Black Officer in a Buffalo Soldier Regiment.* Lincoln: University of Nebraska Press, 2010.

Smith, Amanda Berry. *An Autobiography: The Story of the Lord's Dealings with Mrs. Amanda Smith the Colored Evangelist.* Edited by Henry Louis Gates Jr., with an introduction by Jualynne E. Dodson. New York: Oxford University Press, 1988.

Smith, Charles Spencer. *A History of the African Methodist Episcopal Church: Being a Volume Supplemental to a History of the African Methodist Episcopal Church, by Daniel Alexander Payne, D. D., L.L.D., Late One of its Bishops, Chronicling The Principal Events in the Advance of the African Methodist Episcopal Church from 1856 to 1922.* Philadelphia: Book Concern of the AME Church, 1922.

Smith, Jessie Carney, ed. *Notable Black American Women.* Book 2. Farmington Hills: Thomson-Gale, 1996.

Smith, Valerie. "'Loopholes of Retreat': Architecture and Ideology in Harriet Jacobs' *Incidents in the Life of a Slave Girl.*" In *Reading Black, Reading Feminist: A Critical Anthology,* edited by Henry Louis Gates Jr., 212–26. New York: Meridian Books, 1990.

Stewart, Maria W., Jarena Lee, Julia A. J. Foote, and Virginia W. Broughton, eds. *Spiritual Narratives.* With an introduction by Sue Houchins. Schomburg Library of Nineteenth Century Black Women Writers. New York: Oxford University Press, 1988.

Taylor, Susie King. *Reminiscences of My Life in Camp with the 33d United States Colored Troops Late 1st South Carolina Volunteers.* Boston: The author, 1902.

Thomas, Rhondda Robinson, and Susanna Ashton, eds. *The South Carolina Roots of African American Thought: A Reader.* Columbia: University of South Carolina Press, 2014.

Tindall, George Brown. *South Carolina Negroes, 1877–1900.* Columbia: University of South Carolina Press, 2003. First published in 1952.

Tucker, Spencer C., ed. *The Encyclopedia of the Spanish-American and Philippine-American Wars: A Political, Social, and Military History.* Santa Barbara: ABC-CLIO, 2009.

Updegraff, Marie. "Education Spelled Freedom." In *Stamford, Past and Present.* Stamford: Stamford Bicentennial Committee, 1976. http://www.cslib.org/stamford/pp_ed .htm.

Washington, Margaret, ed. *Narrative of Sojourner Truth.* New York: Vintage Books, 1993.

Washington, Reginald. *Black Family Research: Records of Post-Civil War Federal Agencies at the National Archives.* Washington, DC: National Archives and Records Administration, 2001.

Webber, Mabel Louise, ed. *The South Carolina Historical and Genealogical Magazine.* Baltimore: Williams & Wilkins, 1938.

Weir, Robert, M. *Colonial South Carolina: A History.* Millwood, NY: KTO Press, 1983.

Wesley, John, et al. *A Collection of Hymns, for the Use of the Methodist Episcopal Church, Principally from the Collection of the Rev. John Wesley, A. M. Late Fellow of Lincoln College, Oxford.* New York: George Lane and P. P. Sanford, 1840.

Williams, Heather Andrea. *Self-Taught: African American Education in Slavery and Freedom.* Chapel Hill: University of North Carolina Press, 2005.

Williard, Frances Elizabeth. *Woman and Temperance: or, The Work and Workers of the Women's Christian Temperance Union.* Hartford: James Betts & Co, 1888.

Wilson, Harriet E. *Our Nig, or, Sketches from the Life of a Free Black.* Edited by P. Gabrielle Foreman and Reginald H. Pitts. Penguin Classics. New York: Penguin Books, 2009.

Wineapple, Brenda. *Ecstatic Nation: Confidence, Crisis, and Compromise, 1848–1877.* New York: HarperCollins, 2013.

Wood, Rev. James, comp. *Dictionary of Quotations from Ancient and Modern, English and Foreign Sources.* London: Frederick Warne and Company, 1899.

Wright, Richard R., and John Russell Hawkins, eds. *Centennial Encyclopedia of the African Methodist Episcopal Church.* Vol. 1. Philadelphia: Book Concern of the A.M.E. Church, 1916.

INDEX

Wisconsin Studies in Autobiography

WILLIAM L. ANDREWS
Series Editor

My Generation: Collective Autobiography and Identity Politics
John Downton Hazlett

Jumping the Line: The Adventures and Misadventures of an American Radical
William Herrick

Women, Autobiography, Theory: A Reader
Edited by Sidonie Smith and Julia Watson

The Making of a Chicano Militant: Lessons from Cristal
José Angel Gutiérrez

Rosa: The Life of an Italian Immigrant
Marie Hall Ets

Illumination and Night Glare: The Unfinished Autobiography of Carson McCullers
Carson McCullers
Edited with an introduction by Carlos L. Dews

Who Am I? An Autobiography of Emotion, Mind, and Spirit
Yi-Fu Tuan

The Life and Adventures of Henry Bibb: An American Slave
Henry Bibb
With a new introduction by Charles J. Heglar

Diaries of Girls and Women: A Midwestern American Sampler
Edited by Suzanne L. Bunkers

The Autobiographical Documentary in America
Jim Lane

Caribbean Autobiography: Cultural Identity and Self-Representation
Sandra Pouchet Paquet

How I Became a Human Being: A Disabled Man's Quest for Independence
Mark O'Brien, with Gillian Kendall

*Campaigns of Curiosity: Journalistic Adventures of an American Girl
    in Late Victorian London*
Elizabeth L. Banks
Introduction by Mary Suzanne Schriber and Abbey L. Zink

Mark Twain's Own Autobiography: The Chapters from the "North American Review,"
    second edition
Mark Twain
Edited by Michael J. Kiskis

Graphic Subjects: Critical Essays on Autobiography and Graphic Novels
Edited by Michael A. Chaney

A Muslim American Slave: The Life of Omar Ibn Said
Omar Ibn Said
Translated from the Arabic, edited, and with an introduction by Ala Alryyes

Sister: An African American Life in Search of Justice
Sylvia Bell White and Jody LePage

Identity Technologies: Constructing the Self Online
Edited by Anna Poletti and Julie Rak

Masked: The Life of Anna Leonowens, Schoolmistress at the Court of Siam
Alfred Habegger

We Shall Bear Witness: Life Narratives and Human Rights
Edited by Meg Jensen and Margaretta Jolly

Dear World: Contemporary Uses of the Diary
Kylie Cardell

Words of Witness: Black Women's Autobiography in the Post-"Brown" Era
Angela A. Ards

A Mysterious Life and Calling: From Slavery to Ministry in South Carolina
Reverend Mrs. Charlotte S. Riley
Edited with an introduction by Crystal J. Lucky